AOTEAROA
NEW ZEALAND

ASIA

Gospel and Culture pamphlets:

1. S. Wesley Ariarajah, *An Ongoing Discussion in the Ecumenical Movement*
2. Stan McKay and Janet Silman, *The First Nations of Canada*
3. Ion Bria, *Romania*
4. Noel Davies, *Wales*
5. James Massey, *Panjab*
6. Antonie Wessels, *Secularized Europe*
7. Israel Selvanayagam, *Tamilnadu*
8. Ambrose Moyo, *Zimbabwe*
9. John Pobee, *West Africa*
10. Lewin L. Williams, *The Caribbean*
11. Donald E. Meek, *The Scottish Highlands*
12. Allan K. Davidson, *Aotearoa New Zealand*

GOSPEL AND CULTURES PAMPHLET 12

AOTEAROA NEW ZEALAND

*Defining Moments
in the Gospel-Culture Encounter*

Allan K. Davidson

WCC Publications, Geneva

Cover design: Edwin Hassink/WCC
Cover illustration: Found along northern coastlines in Aotearoa New Zealand, the Pohutukawa, with dark green foliage and brilliant red flower which blooms in December, is called the "New Zealand Christmas tree" and is an indigenous symbol for the Advent season (photo Margaret Davidson).

ISBN 2-8254-1205-8

© 1996 WCC Publications, World Council of Churches,
150 route de Ferney, 1211 Geneva 2, Switzerland

No. 12 in the Gospel and Cultures series

Printed in Switzerland

Table of Contents

vii	INTRODUCTION
1	1. 1814: MAORI AND MISSIONARIES
14	2. 1840: COLONIAL CHRISTIANITY
26	3. 1893: RESHAPING CHURCH AND SOCIETY
36	4. 1940: GOD'S OWN COUNTRY
48	5. 1990: THE CHALLENGE OF CULTURES
58	6. ENDINGS AND BEGINNINGS

Introduction

The meeting of cultures

Aotearoa is the commonly accepted Maori name for New Zealand. The Maori, a Polynesian people, began settling this land in the southwest Pacific over one thousand years ago. Coming in their *waka* (canoes), they made this *whenua* (land), a country of two major and many smaller islands, their own. They named its features, identifying themselves as *tangata whenua* (people of the land), each *hapu* (clan) and *iwi* (tribe) defined by its own mountain and river.

Maori adapted the Polynesian cosmology they brought with them in order to give meaning to the world in which they lived. *Rangi* (the sky father) and *Papa* (the earth mother) became the parents of other *atua* (spiritual beings). The separation of *Rangi* from *Papa* led to the creation of men and women. Maui the fisherman brought up *Te Ika a Maui* (the fish of Maui) from the southern oceans and the North Island of Aotearoa was born. Through metaphor, poetry and story the rich mythological tradition of the Maori provided them with a strong sense of identity and belonging within Aotearoa.

Maori developed a sophisticated religious framework with their own rich concepts such as *mauri*, the life principle of the individual; *wairua*, the spiritual dimension of life; *mana*, the power and prestige associated with a person that was both given and gained; *tapu*, the sacred force controlling behaviour; and *noa*, the ordinary and acceptable, in which people were free from *tapu*. *Karakia* (prayers or incantations) were significant in the regulation of the sacred and secular, with *tohunga* (priests) playing an important role in these. In their relationships with one another, primacy was given to the *whanau* (family) and *iwi* (the tribe), with *rangatira* (chiefs) and *kaumatua* (elders) given special respect and leadership. *Whakapapa* (tribal lineage) was emphasized. Maori developed a strong warrior tradition and intertribal conflict could be fierce but tribal confederations and intermarriage also resulted in tribal alliances.

Maori adapted their tropical Polynesian lifestyle to the temperate climate and diverse landscape where they made their homes. Their culture integrated the world in which they lived with their own *kawa*, ceremonies to regulate life and the rites of passage. Maori had their own *atua*, their lesser spirits and even, some would say, *Io*, a supreme being. Aotearoa was their home and their land.

The arrival of the first European explorers led to a clash of two worlds. Abel Tasman, a Dutchman, and the two ships under his command made brief contact with Maori and their land in 1642. This first contact was impeded by cross-cultural misunderstanding, resulting in the death of four Dutch sailors and an aggressive European reaction. The area the Maori called Taitapu was renamed by the Dutch *Moordenaers Baij*, "Murderers Bay", later renamed Golden Bay. The name *Zeelandia Nova*, New Zealand, was given to Tasman's "discovery" by map-makers in Europe. The brief encounter resulted in Maori being described as savage and uncivilized. The imposition of the European world on the Maori world — New Zealand on Aotearoa — had begun.

Captain James Cook's crew, the next Europeans to encounter Maori, also made an inauspicious beginning. In 1769 they arrived at Turanganui on the east coast of the North Island. Despite Cook's peaceful intentions, the first contacts resulted in the death and wounding of a number of Maori. Cook withdrew from the place, where he had hoped to gain fresh water and provisions, naming the area Poverty Bay. Through his three extensive voyages, Cook, more than anyone else, was responsible for putting what was now called New Zealand on the European map.

During the following decades European contact with Maori was largely exploitative as whalers, sealers and traders used New Zealand as a place for refreshment, and to gain timber and flax (used for rope-making), while Maori sought iron and European goods. Some "Pakeha" (the name given by Maori to Europeans) took up residence in New Zealand. There were occasional outbursts of violence, for example in

1809 when the ship *Boyd* was sacked and most of its passengers and crew killed, probably as a Maori response to indignities meted out to a local chief.

Maori appreciation of European culture was initially limited. While Cook and some of his companions and other early explorers were men of principle and good intentions, their crews, the whalers, traders and some escaped convicts from Australia represented the rougher side of European life. There was little attempt to give expression to overt Christian values in these initial contacts. Missionary motivation, which was significant for the Spanish and Portuguese explorers in the 15th to the 17th centuries, often with disastrous consequences, played little part in European contact with New Zealand before the 19th century.

Some Maori sought experience of the wider world as sailors on European ships. They brought back knowledge of the strange ways of other worlds and peoples. European goods (particularly iron) and the introduction of muskets resulted in a flourishing trade in the early 19th century, particularly in the north, sometimes with devastating results as Maori undertook reprisal raids on their traditional enemies. The introduction of European diseases such as tuberculosis, whooping cough, diphtheria, influenza and measles, to which Maori had no natural immunity, had a profound impact on them. Throughout the 19th century the old and the young were particularly affected, with the consequent loss of those who were the bearers of tradition and those who carried the future of the race. The Maori population in the 19th century dropped between 50 and 75 percent. Many thought they were a dying people.

An appreciation of the richness of Maori culture and the nature of early European and Maori interaction is an important backdrop for the discussion of gospel and culture in Aotearoa New Zealand. The use of the two names, Aotearoa and New Zealand, indicates the significance of the indigenous and exotic dimensions of this history. Before the coming of the missionaries and the formal presentation of the gospel message, Maori had their own ways of giving meaning to life. Maori already had experience of interaction with European culture, albeit in incomplete forms, before the missionaries began to try to evangelize them. Maori sailors returning from Australia and elsewhere brought knowledge of European religion and ways of worship. The coming of missionaries brought another dimension to the cultural encounter which was already under way between Maori and Pakeha.

The second major dimension in the history of gospel and culture in Aotearoa New Zealand began with the arrival of increasing numbers of Pakeha settlers and their churches after 1840. For settlers coming from the northern hemisphere intent on improving their way of life and providing a better future for their children, the church provided a link between the old world from which they came and the new world in which they lived. How far the churches adapted to their new context is a question which has contemporary significance as Christians face issues of identity and the relevance of the gospel to late 20th-century life in Aotearoa New Zealand.

Since it is not possible to give a detailed history within the scope of this booklet, we shall look instead at several defining moments in the relationship between gospel and culture in Aotearoa New Zealand, pivotal historical events which provide a framework for interpreting the interaction of gospel and culture and point to some of the themes which have been interwoven into the fabric of the story of the peoples who have lived in Aotearoa New Zealand.

Some of these themes have universal dimensions, such as the interaction of the gospel, which was already shaped by its own cultural containers brought by the missionaries, with the culture and religious world of indigenous peoples. The interaction of European settlers, colonial cultures and societies with "the people of the land" or First Nation people in other parts of the world, contain similarities. But these themes also point to contrasts with the experiences of other countries. The history of Aotearoa New Zealand has its own uniqueness which illuminates the interaction of gospel and culture here.

Even the terms "gospel" and "culture" are problematic. "Gospel" was defined and used in different ways. The missionaries identified it with their understanding of the good news that they brought to Maori. For the settlers the gospel was shaped and determined by their own particular denominational histories and traditions. These different versions of the gospel were themselves defined and shaped by the variety of cultures which contained and expressed them. Throughout history the gospel has always been expressed historically and contextually. It is never without a cultural context. At the same time the question of the gospel behind the gospel — what the good news of Jesus Christ was or is and how far the different versions of the gospel proclaimed throughout history have reflected or distorted this — is open to continuing debate. This publication does not try to describe the gospel of Jesus Christ. It is more concerned with the historical processes involved in bringing the gospel(s) already defined by culture(s) to a different historical and geographical context and the consequent interactions.

The understanding of "culture" reflected in these essays points to the ways in which people from different backgrounds give meaning to life. No one culture is seen as superior to any another. Within the English, Scottish, Irish and other cultures brought to New Zealand there are points of similarity and dissimilarity. The gospel as it was expressed through different Christian denominations had its own character and identity, so that each of these denominations operated almost as subcultures or even religious cultures.

Throughout this book Maori terms have been used, with English explanations, to help emphasize the particularity and interaction of cultures. As a country young in terms of nationhood, Aotearoa New Zealand has been and is involved in a search for identity. For Maori, with their own long history of residence in Aotearoa and their tribal affiliations and associations with the land, this issue of identity has its own special character. For Pakeha and all subsequent migrants the issue of identity is coloured by their own history and particular experiences. For the churches their identity is deeply involved in questions relating to gospel and culture. These chapters are an attempt by a Pakeha historian to understand aspects of the historical dimensions relating to this, in the hope of shedding light on this ecclesiological search for identity as the churches approach a new millennium.

1. 1814: Maori and Missionaries

> On Sunday morning, when I was upon deck, I saw the English flag flying, which was a pleasing sight in New Zealand. I considered it as the signal and the dawn of civilization, liberty and religion, in that dark and benighted land. I never viewed the British colours with more gratification; and flattered myself they would never be removed, till the natives of that island enjoyed all the happiness of British subjects...
>
> It being Christmas day, I preached from the second chapter of St Luke's gospel, and tenth verse — *Behold! I bring you glad tidings of great joy, &c.* The Natives told Duaterra [Ruatara] that they could not understand what I meant. He replied, that they were not to mind that now, for they would understand by and by; and that he would explain my meaning as far as he could. [1]

Christmas Day 1814 was a defining moment in the history of gospel and culture in Aotearoa New Zealand. On that day Samuel Marsden, Anglican chaplain to the New South Wales colony in Australia, preached at Oihi Bay in the Bay of Islands, New Zealand. While possibly not the first Christian service in New Zealand, it marked the beginning of missionary work and the settlement of missionaries at Rangihoua.

The above extract from Marsden's account of the day's proceedings clearly reflects the close association he made between his Christian commitment and his English identity. From the outset of Christian involvement in Aotearoa New Zealand, gospel and culture were inextricably intertwined. This is seen in the pleasure Marsden took at the sight of the English flag flying in New Zealand as the beginning of "civilization, liberty and religion" and his looking forward to Maori becoming "British subjects".

Often seen as the patriarch of Christianity in New Zealand, Marsden was, however, an ambiguous figure. In Australia, where he was a successful entrepreneur and farmer, he also had the reputation of being a harsh, unforgiving magistrate. But Marsden was committed to the spread of Christianity, supporting the pioneering work of the London

Missionary Society in the Pacific and making attempts, albeit unsuccessful, to evangelize Aborigines in Australia. He was a product of the 18th-century evangelical revivals, and his uncritical identification of Christianity with British civilization and national identity reflected the evangelical worldview.

Marsden persuaded the Church Missionary Society (CMS), founded in 1799 as a voluntary society within the Church of England, to look to New Zealand as one of its early areas of missionary endeavour. He argued that "nothing, in my opinion, can pave the way for the introduction of the gospel, but civilization".[2] To promote this end he secured the appointment of three artisan missionaries by the CMS, hoping they would introduce their crafts to Maori as well as teach them the truths of Christianity.

Missionary beginnings were not a one-sided English affair. The extract cited above refers to Ruatara, who explained what he could of Marsden's sermon. Ruatara was from the area where the CMS began its mission. He spent a number of years working on whaling ships, going as far as England. Marsden first met Ruatara in Australia in 1806. In 1809 when Marsden was returning from England to Australia he found Ruatara on the same ship. Ruatara had been mistreated and was in ill health. Marsden befriended him and during the voyage began learning Maori. At his home at Parramatta in Australia, Marsden gave Ruatara hospitality and helped him gain knowledge of European farming methods and carpentry.

Ruatara played a crucial role in helping to begin the CMS mission in New Zealand in 1814. He has been described as *"Te ara mo te Rongopai*, the gateway for the gospel". Sadly, he died soon after Marsden returned to Australia in March 1815; and the protection and support he gave were taken over by another chief, Hongi Hika, who was more interested in the material advantages coming from his association with the missionaries. With the help of newly acquired muskets, Hongi engaged in aggressive campaigns against his traditional enemies in the early 1820s, upsetting the balance of power in the region and making missionary work very difficult.

For the first missionaries, Thomas Kendall, William Hall, John King and their families, life was often precarious. British Protestant missionary activity was still in its first generation and there was no immediate tradition to call upon to help with missionary methodology. Missionaries were learning how to go about evangelization in what were to them alien cultures and contexts. Communication with mission authorities in England usually took over a year. Marsden's visits from Australia were intermittent and his advice was not informed by on-the-spot experience.

The mission was not helped by personality conflicts. Missionaries lacked the critical tools to understand how closely their own Christianity was enmeshed with their own culture. Marsden's view of New Zealand as a "dark and benighted land" reflected the evangelical dismissal of indigenous cultures as inherently unredeemable without the importation of Christianity in its English cultural form. Initial attempts at formal schooling for Maori were unproductive. The sedentary form of education made little sense to them, since they saw no obvious benefits to be gained from it.

An important step was taken when Kendall began to master the Maori language. Together with Hongi and another chief, Waikato, he went to England in 1820, where Professor Samuel Lee at Cambridge University helped to construct the first Maori grammar, published later that year.

Kendall also began to make significant attempts to understand Maori cosmology and religious beliefs, though these were distorted by his view that Maori originated in Egypt. Religious studies, linguistics and cross-cultural ethnography, to which missionaries made important contributions in the 19th century, were still being forced into interpretative frameworks that reflected the European, biblical and Graeco-Roman worldviews. Sadly Kendall's pioneering work was terminated following his dismissal from the mission in 1823 and his departure from New Zealand in 1825.

In 1823 Henry Williams arrived to lead the CMS work. A former naval officer, he brought discipline to the mission and directed its energies away from Marsden's emphasis on civilizing to evangelization. Williams acquired considerable status for his work as a forceful peacemaker among conflicting Maori groups. Together with his colleagues he broke the missionaries' dependency on Maori for food and transport, developing a farm station and building a sailing ship. He was helped by other long-serving missionaries, their wives and families, who became an integral part of the Maori communities where they lived. Henry's brother William arrived in 1826. An Oxford graduate, William helped translate the New Testament (completed in 1837) and *The Book of Common Prayer*.

The gospel brought by the CMS missionaries and by the Wesleyan Methodists, who commenced work in New Zealand in 1822, initially in close cooperation with the CMS, reflected the evangelical experience which shaped their missionary vocation. Individual conversion following conviction of sin was a critical stage in the spiritual development of an evangelical. They looked to reproduce in Maori what had been a turning-point in their own lives.

In New Zealand the missionaries encountered a people whose identity was intimately involved with their membership of family, clan and tribal groups. The idea of an individual making a decision which would lead to separation from others was alien. The missionary view of salvation had little to offer to Maori. According to Augustus Earle, a visitor to New Zealand in 1827-28, missionary teaching about eternal punishment and the torments of hell led Maori to respond that "'they were quite sure such a place could only be made for white faces, for they had no men half wicked enough in New Zealand to be sent there'". When they were told that "'all men' would be condemned" they "burst into a loud laugh, declaring 'they would have nothing to do with a

God who delighted in such cruelties; and then (as a matter of right) hoped the missionary would give them each a blanket for having taken the trouble of listening to him so patiently'".[3]

Missionary attitudes towards Sunday worship and "the Sabbath" as a day of rest, free from all commerce and work, were also a source of astonishment among Maori. They appreciated the nature of *tapu*, prohibitions of activity, and the sense of the holy or awesome in worship, but religious observances for Maori were related to specific activities, such as preparation for battle, cutting down a tree or marking the death of someone, rather than a specially designated day. Drawing on their understanding of their own meeting places as *tapu* or holy, Maori had great respect for church buildings. When they gathered together with the missionaries for public worship, Earle noted, "they always behaved with the utmost decorum when admitted into the house where the ceremony takes place".[4]

In order to convert Maori, evangelical missionaries introduced their own theological framework and patterns of worship into the Maori world in ways that Maori could respond to and accept. The dynamics associated with Maori acceptance of Christianity, however, were much more complex than a simple Maori assent to the missionaries' message. The gospel brought by the missionaries was clothed in evangelical assumptions and English cultural prejudices. Within the missionaries' message, however, were gospel teachings such as love of enemies, which came as a challenge to traditional warrior values.

Maori were responding to the missionaries out of their own worldview and way of life. Throughout the second half of the 1820s changes were observed taking place within Maori society originating from Maori themselves, although often in response to missionary teaching. George Clarke, a CMS missionary, reported in January 1826 that "the native taboos [*tapu*] begin to be broken, and the rising generation no longer feel themselves bound to wear the shackles of their fathers". He noted examples such as the planting of sweet potatoes without prayers and how Maori were "gaining a knowledge of the theory of religion" and making inquiries "to know who that Great Saviour is that we so much talk to them about".[5]

Historians have debated intensely why many Maori accepted Christianity in the 1830s and 1840s after initially rejecting it. Some point to the impact of war-weariness, depopulation caused by disease, fighting and new ways of life, and cultural confusion as old patterns of belief were challenged and were unable to respond. In this context the missionary message offered a new worldview and understanding of salvation.

Other historians have argued that trade and European goods led Maori to associate with missionaries. Maori were very entrepreneurial, growing potatoes and wheat and raising pigs to trade with Europeans. In the 1840s and 1850s they built their own flour mills and sailing vessels to engage in trade as far away as Australia. Within their own culture, prosperity was undergirded by religious rituals; and the acceptance of Christianity represented a logical development as Maori became more closely involved in the European world. But these factors were by no means universal throughout the country and by themselves do not adequately explain why Maori became Christians so quickly in such large numbers.

Two factors which clearly contributed to the spread of Christianity were the impact of literacy and the activities of indigenous evangelists. William Yate spoke in 1835 about "the thirst for knowledge which has been excited among the New Zealanders... Everyone now wishes to learn to read and write."[6] The translation of parts of the New Testament and the distribution of the first printed copies elicited a response which surprised the missionaries. Like the computer in contemporary society, literacy became the tool to give access to new knowledge; and for the Maori this new knowledge available in their own language was exclusively religious.

The printed text itself was seen as *tapu* or holy. The medium became part of the message.

Spontaneously, Maori who had learned something of the missionaries' message and had some acquaintance with reading and writing shared this with others. Among them were some who had been captured in battle and taken to the north, where they had encountered the missionaries' teaching and come to admire the gospel of peace and reconciliation which they shared. Arriving in villages for the first time, missionaries found that their message had gone ahead of them.

Throughout the 1830s and 1840s both the CMS and Wesleyan Methodists expanded from their bases in the north and tried to incorporate Maori Christians under the umbrella of their missions, catechizing and baptizing Maori and training teachers and catechists. The impact of the gospel on Maori and their culture worked at different levels. With their great ability to memorize, Maori learned by heart large parts of the liturgy and, as it became available in translation, the Bible. Formal rhetorical speeches were significant in Maori culture and these were increasingly infused with biblical allusions, sometimes in ways which perplexed the missionaries. Great interest was shown, for example, in biblical genealogy which was not surprising given the importance of *whakapapa* (lineage) in establishing Maori identity. At baptism many Maori adopted biblical names in Maori forms.

Changes also took place in Maori society. The missionaries condemned concubinage and required monogamy of those who were baptized. Some leading chiefs chose to retain one wife and were married according to Christian rites. The emphasis on peacemaking and reconciliation between conflicting tribes and the ending of the cycle of *utu* (payback) was encouraged. In some cases old scores were still settled by warfare, but practices such as the use of prisoners as slaves were ended.

The Maori response to the gospel was complex and varied. George Clarke estimated in 1845 that out of a total Maori population of 110,000 some 64,000 were regularly attending mission services. How many of these Maori Christians met the missionaries' expectations is difficult to estimate. There is evidence that many Maori associated with the missions as sodality groups. Some individuals clearly impressed the missionaries by their theological knowledge and spiritual example. Other examples, such as Papahurihia in the early 1830s, indicate that Maori were assimilating the missionaries' message and European influences within their own culture, giving rise to new religious movements which were syncretistic and early instances of indigenous theological responses to Christianity.

An element of rivalry was introduced into this spread of Christianity with the arrival in 1838 of French Roman Catholic missionaries from the Society of Mary, the Marists, under the leadership of Bishop Jean-Baptiste François Pompallier. Thus the Protestant-Catholic antagonisms of the northern hemisphere, inflamed by the Reformation and subsequent history, along with nationalistic rivalries between the British and French, were introduced into Aotearoa New Zealand. The gospel brought by the Marists reflected a French Catholic culture. The harassment of Catholics by the Protestant missionaries led to the visit of a French naval vessel *La Héroïne* to the Bay of Islands, and to a show of force which elsewhere in the Pacific at this time had checked Protestant attacks on Catholics. The Sunday after the ship's arrival "mass was celebrated on the deck of the vessel amidst all the pomp and splendour at the ship's command" with flags flying and the gunners going through their exercises at the elevation of the host.[7] For Maori the varieties of Christianity they were now persuaded to accept resulted in some confusion and their division into denominations, often along traditional tribal lines.

The missionaries and their supporters in England were concerned with more than the salvation of souls. The evangelical movement was closely aligned with humanitarian concerns such as the abolition of the slave trade and slavery. There was a growing concern about the rights of indigenous peoples. Contrasting pictures were drawn between the European settlement in the Bay of Islands at Kororareka, which was referred to by Marsden during his last visit in 1837 as the place where "Satan maintains his dominion without molestation",[8] and the mission headquarters at Paihia. Missionaries complained about the way in which European immorality undermined their teaching, and began to campaign for legal constraints to check the worst excesses of Pakeha behaviour.

Missionaries played a crucial role in Maori becoming British subjects in 1840. Protestant missionaries initially opposed colonization, two of them witnessing a Maori Declaration of independence in 1835. The missionaries were persuaded by a variety of factors, including the beginning of large-scale European migration to New Zealand and the fear of French annexation, to support actions to bring New Zealand under British sovereignty. Henry Williams helped translate the treaty of Waitangi, the proceedings at Waitangi in February 1840 when the treaty was introduced to Maori, and along with other missionaries secured Maori signatures to the document throughout the country.

The treaty was drawn up by Captain Hobson, who became the first governor. It recognized the 1835 Declaration, but there was confusion between the Maori and English texts of the treaty. The Maori text, which most chiefs signed, ceded the governance of the land to the British crown while guaranteeing the chiefs supremacy over their land and property. In the English text sovereignty was ceded to the crown and Maori were guaranteed possession of their lands.

A spirited debate took place at Waitangi before the treaty was signed. Hone Heke, a leading chief, saw the treaty as "a good thing — it is even as the word of God", and encouraged other Maori to follow the advice of the missionaries.[9] Some chiefs saw it as "a special kind of covenant with the Queen, a bond with all the spiritual connotations of the biblical covenants; there would be many tribes, including the British, but all would be equal under God".[10] William Colenso, a CMS missionary, warned however that Maori did not fully understand the treaty and could later blame missionaries for not fully informing them. Bishop Pompallier stood somewhat aloof from these British proceedings, although at his insistence guarantees of religious freedom were given to Protestant, Catholic and Maori faiths and customs.

In traditional Maori culture, law and religion were part of the overall framework of society. The involvement of missionaries in religious and moral teaching, agricultural development and political issues could easily be understood by Maori in traditional terms. But the relationship between the missionaries and the government authorities both before and after the treaty was ambiguous. The influence missionaries had before 1840 came from their involvement in Maori society and the European political vacuum in New Zealand. After 1840 their authority was quickly undermined and marginalized by the growth of the colonial government and the influence of the increasing settler population with its own concerns. The settler pressure for more and more land conflicted with the missionaries' attempts to safeguard their own interests and to protect Maori.

Following the signing of the treaty of Waitangi, Maori were faced with challenges to their sovereignty. Confrontation over land at Wairau in the northeast of the South Island in 1843 resulted in the death of 24 settlers and 4 Maori. In 1844-45 the Northern War in the Bay of Islands area resulted in a series of inconclusive battles. Hone Heke, attacking a symbol of British sovereignty, cut down the flagpole at Kororareka four times. In 1846 the missionaries successfully protested against the British colonial secretary's attempt to declare all unoccupied Maori land as "waste land". But the status of some of the missionaries, including Henry Williams, was undermined by the governor's attack on their own personal landholdings.

Throughout the 1840s and 1850s missionaries noted that many Maori were not as enthusiastic about the church as they would have wished and that a great deal of energy was going into commercial enterprises. Missionaries had mixed success in developing educational programmes which encouraged Maori development and leadership. Bishop George Selwyn, who arrived in New Zealand in 1842 to head up the Anglican Church, attempted to develop a broadly based educational institution, but by 1853 it had collapsed. His failure to ordain Maori to the priesthood delayed the development of indigenous leadership.

Maori developed their own political structures, notably through the King movement in the central North Island, as they attempted to withstand Pakeha pressure on their land. The outbreak of war in Taranaki in 1860, following an illegal land purchase by the Crown, prompted a vigorous defence of Maori rights by leading Anglicans. The Waikato War which began in 1863, however, resulted in little support for Maori. Maori assertion of sovereignty and the defence of their land was seen as conflicting with the authority of the government. Since Bishop Selwyn and some missionaries acted as chaplains to the British forces, they lost credibility in the eyes of Maori and were thus unable to act as mediators or peacemakers.

The emergence of vigorous Maori religious movements at this time represented a rejection of the missionary churches rather than of Christianity itself. This was seen in the execution of C.S. Volkner, a CMS missionary, by Maori in 1865, because of his supposed association with some of the atrocities Maori had suffered and his actions as a government informant or spy.

The interweaving of biblical themes within the movements led by Te Ua Haumene, Te Kooti Rikirangi and Te Whiti o Rongomai looked to the deliverance of their people from what were seen as oppressive forces. Te Ua's movement began with peaceful intentions but became caught up in the violence of the wars, Volkner's death and the destruction of the mission station at Turanganui. Te Kooti's movement began with *utu*, seen in violent reprisals, but was transformed into the Ringatu Church with its use of the Psalms, monthly worship and reinforcement of Maori values of *whanau* (family), and indigenous culture. Te Whiti, together with Tohu, in the face of land confiscations in the 1870s and 1880s, used strategies of civil disobedience and pacifism.

These brief descriptions can be only suggestive of how some Maori responded to the pressures they faced. The repeated accusation brought against the missionaries was that of teaching Maori to lift up their eyes to heaven while keeping their own eyes turned down to the land.[11] The gospel Marsden helped to introduce contributed to Maori becoming British subjects, but the results were often disastrous for Maori. Colenso, reflecting in 1868 on the serious depopulation among Maori, concluded that "apart from any spiritual benefit... it would have been far better for the New Zealanders *as a people* if they had never seen a European".[12]

The role of missionaries in any society is mixed and open to a variety of interpretations. In the New Zealand context they were one influence among many, albeit a major one in the early years. The gospel they brought reflected the worlds from which they came. What they were not prepared for was how Maori took the gospel into their own culture on their own terms. While Maori had become British subjects they retained their strong sense of identity as Maori. The gospel which they acquired reinforced this through the variety of forms of Maori Christianity which they adopted. Some of these were aligned with the missionary churches while others were, in missionary terms, heterodox. Almost despite the missionaries, Maori in some notable instances creatively adapted their carving, art and architecture, their speeches and songs, to express the impact of Christianity within their culture. The relation between gospel and culture for Maori in the 19th century was dynamic and complex.

NOTES

[1] A.K. Davidson and P.J. Lineham, *Transplanted Christianity: Documents Illustrating Aspects of New Zealand Church History*, Palmerston North, Dunmore Press, 1989, 2nd ed., p.28.

[2] *Ibid.*, p.26.
[3] *Ibid.*, p.37.
[4] *Ibid.*
[5] *Ibid.*, p.43.
[6] *Ibid.*, p.44.
[7] J.J. Wilson, *The Church in New Zealand: Memoirs of the Early Days*, Dunedin, Tablet, 1910, p.12.
[8] J.R. Elder, *The Letters and Journals of Samuel Marsden 1765-1838*, Dunedin, Coulls Somerville Wilkie, 1932, p.523.
[9] W. Colenso, *The Authentic and Genuine History of the Signing of the Treaty of Waitangi...*, Wellington, Government Printer, 1890, p.26.
[10] C. Orange, *The Treaty of Waitangi*, Wellington, Allen and Unwin, p.57.
[11] Davidson and Lineham, *op. cit.*, p.148.
[12] W. Colenso, "On the Maori Races of New Zealand", in *Transactions and Proceedings of the New Zealand Institute*, Vol. 1, 1868, p.75.

2. 1840: Colonial Christianity

> The Roman Catholics are on the alert, and we have had a visit, in consequence, from the bishop, who celebrated mass twice, and was treated with the greatest deference and respect by the officials. The Church of England also, for which I bear the highest respect, is exerting, as I perceive by the public papers, every nerve to acquire a predominancy; and not a few of her members here have frequently displayed an arrogant jealousy of the Church of Scotland. I trust, I earnestly hope she will not remain apathetic, that she will not neglect one of the noblest opportunities ever afforded her of promulgating the doctrines of the gospel, and of establishing in this far isle of ocean the simple but at the same time sublime form of worship belonging to the covenant, blood-sealed Kirk of our Fathers.[1]

John Macfarlane, the first resident Presbyterian minister in New Zealand, sent this appeal back to the Colonial Committee of the Church of Scotland asking for the appointment of additional Presbyterian ministers to help provide ministry for the growing number of Scottish settlers in the country. His arrival at Wellington in February 1840 was part of another defining moment in New Zealand history, the beginning of what can be called the settler or colonial churches.

The New Zealand Land Company formed in England promoted the systematic colonization of New Zealand. It dispatched an expedition to New Zealand in 1839 to buy up land as cheaply as possible from Maori and to prepare for the arrival of migrants. The British government, largely as a result of active missionary and humanitarian lobbies, was concerned about uncontrolled colonization and decided to send Captain Hobson to New Zealand to acquire, with the help of Maori chiefs, sovereignty over the country and control of land transactions, and to make provisions for Maori welfare. The treaty of Waitangi, described in the previous chapter, resulted from this.

From the outset there were tensions between the missionaries and those leading the colonizing movement. The missionaries were committed to working with and for Maori and were seen by the colonizers as barriers to their acquisition of land for settlement. In 1840, when the treaty of Waitangi was signed, it was estimated that there were only some 2000 Pakeha settlers in the country. Within twenty years Maori were outnumbered by Pakeha and the Maori population was in serious decline. The emerging colonial society was largely antagonistic towards Maori rights and interests.

The role of the church in a developing colonial context was fraught with all manner of difficulties. Primary among these, although seldom recognized, was its relationship to the indigenous people. Macfarlane was partially aware of this, noting that "British colonization... forms one of the darkest pages in our national annals". He called for the colonization of New Zealand to "be conducted on Christian principles; let the just rights of the aborigines be respected, their hereditary prejudices dealt with gently".[2]

For migrants coming to New Zealand in the 19th century, pragmatic self-interest was the main motivating force. Religious interests, if they were present at all, were largely secondary. The new settlers were concerned about improving themselves and making a better future for their children. Indigenous rights were the concern only of the idealists or those like the missionaries who identified their life's work with the Maori.

Notions of the superiority of British civilization, reinforced by prejudices against native peoples as uncivilized, produced a sense of dominance that found expression in paternalism and racism. In the second half of the 19th century these attitudes were reinforced by social Darwinism. Alfred Newman, a medical doctor in Wellington, gave expression to these views in 1881 in a paper on the causes of the decline of the Maori population, concluding: "Taking all things into consideration, the disappearance of the race is scarcely subject for much regret. They are dying out in a quick, easy way, and are being supplanted by a superior race."[3]

Notions of racial superiority received little challenge from the colonial churches. This points to a second dimension of the challenge facing churches in colonial societies. The form of ministry they adopted was shaped largely by a chaplaincy or pastoral model. Ministers who came to New Zealand were often faced with scattered communities, with people in isolated rural areas developing farms out of the bush. In the goldfields of the 1860s miners were often very transient. Ministry in the colonial context was driven by a desire to draw people together for worship and to provide pastoral care at the critical times of life. Maintaining stipendiary ministry was often a struggle, with support from the local people combined with grants from the national church, which in turn looked to "home" or British financial aid. Pioneering ministry usually involved travelling by horseback long distances and often, given the geography and climate of the country, under difficult conditions. After paying the clergy, financial resources were directed towards building churches, erecting residences for ministers and supporting education.

Particularly in the North Island in the second half of the century, clergy were ministering to people who gained their livelihood from land that had been confiscated or alienated from Maori. The prosperity of the whole society depended largely on its agricultural foundation and the use of land. There was little expression given to a prophetic voice within the colonial churches. Apart from the notable protests of the Anglican and missionary lobby over the taking of Maori land before the wars of the 1860s there was an almost deafening silence from the colonial churches in the face of what were often highly dubious land transactions by the government. The colonial culture and context helped to shape the kind of gospel preached in colonial society.

As the quotation with which this chapter begins illustrates, denominations were challenged to provide ministry to their own members in colonial societies. In his first sermon in New Zealand, John Macfarlane took as his text Psalm 137:5-6:

> If I forget thee, O Jerusalem, let my right hand forget her cunning. If I do not remember thee, let my tongue cleave to the roof of my mouth; if I prefer not Jerusalem above my chief joy.

There is an identification here with the Israelites in exile in Babylon remaining faithful to the memory of their worship in Jerusalem. The early migrants were faced with the same question as the exilic community: how to sing the Lord's song in a strange land.

The relationship of gospel and culture throughout history has been influenced by the geographical contexts in which the gospel has been presented. The liturgical year, for example, bears the mark of the northern hemisphere, with Easter coinciding with spring and the renewal of nature and Christmas falling during the midwinter solstice, with many aspects shaped by pre-Christian influences. In the southern hemisphere, where seasons are reversed and the world turned upside down, there was a transplantation of northern hemisphere patterns of thinking and acting which now seems incongruous.

The gospel message about incarnation, redemption and resurrection expressed in the Christmas and Easter stories was interwoven with customs that originated in the particular historical and geographical contexts from which the migrants to New Zealand came. Charlotte Godley, reflecting on her first Christmas in New Zealand in 1850, complained that "it was very unlike Christmas Day, so *hot*, even when we went to the early service and communion at 7:30". Their church and house were decorated with New Zealand greenery, but she poignantly noted that they "will not last, like our good holly and ivy and laurel, till Twelfth Night".[4] Halfway around the world from her place of origin, Charlotte Godley, like most migrants, was deeply influenced by the world from which she came. Singing the Lord's song in a strange land meant singing it in the same way you sang it at home even if some aspects were no longer appropriate.

Churches by nature are conservative bodies passing on the traditions which have shaped them and performing the rituals which they have inherited. Migrant communities often look to their churches for a point of security and safety in their new world. The church is the one place where they can sing the songs of Zion in the same way they sang them in the places they came from. In reproducing themselves in new contexts churches therefore often transplant their ways of worship and give little thought to their new context. For Roman Catholics the Tridentine mass, for Anglicans *The Book of Common Prayer*, for Presbyterians *The Shorter Catechism* and *Westminister Confession of Faith*, for Methodists the notes and sermons of John Wesley and the hymns of Charles Wesley, were among some of the distinctive treasures that they brought with them.

But the new context forced some changes and adaptations — seen for example in church buildings. The material at hand in New Zealand was timber. Although the architectural shape of the building reflected the traditions from which people came, the use of timber rather than stone or brick brought a distinctively Aotearoa New Zealand character to them.

The denominational landscape was also very different. The largest proportion of migrants were English, followed by Scots and then Irish. The Church of England was the largest denomination, with its membership reaching 53 percent of the population in 1851 and settling down to just over 41 percent at the end of the century. Presbyterians averaged 23 percent of the population throughout the last thirty years of the century, Roman Catholics some 14 percent and Methodists 9 percent. Denominational affiliation was influenced by place of origin and this contributed to people's sense of identity. Migrants usually thought of "home" as the place from which they came, even if they never went back there.

Within these denominations there was also some diversity. While the Irish became the largest group of Roman Catholics, the distinctive French beginnings of the New Zealand church continued to help shape it throughout the 19th century. For a time, Catholics from Germany who settled at Puhoi had their own German-speaking priest. Presbyterians came not only from Scotland but also England, Ireland and Wales. They also reflected the varieties of Presbyterian churches which resulted from the divisions and strife within Scottish Presbyterianism.

The Disruption in 1843, which led to the split between the Church of Scotland and the Free Church, also found expression in New Zealand. The Lay Association of Members of the Free Church of Scotland was involved in the settlement of Otago and Southland, the southern part of the country. Under the leadership of the Rev. Thomas Burns and Captain William Cargill they wanted to establish a Free Church colony that would be a "Geneva of the Antipodes". When charged with narrowness and bigotry Burns replied, "We are not exclusive — we are only *special* — we only wish to secure for our little community the very delightful privileges of internal harmony and Christian unity as far as we can — we by no means wish to *exclude* you from the same privileges we are in quest of — go ye and do as we are doing."[5]

Within the New Zealand context it was not possible to isolate religious communities from one another and develop a New England Puritan theocracy. Pluralism, the coexistence of different denominational groupings, was a factor in shaping the religious landscape. For example, Canterbury, a Church of England settlement begun in 1850, was diluted by non-Anglican influences. At the same time the distinctive contributions of Presbyterians and Anglicans to their respective communities were significant in helping shape their identity. In Dunedin, the largest settlement in the Otago area, which became known as "the Edinburgh of the South", the Presbyterian emphasis on education was reflected in the establishment of the first public high schools and university in the country. In Canterbury the Anglican impact was seen in the very English Christchurch, with its four squares named after Anglican bishops and the central place given to the cathedral which became the hub of the city.

The religious landscape was by no means uniform throughout the country; there were also distinctive minorities. Lutherans from Germany were among the early colonists in the Moutere area. Scandinavian settlers in the Wairarapa and Manawatu were also predominantly Lutheran. There were also a number of French Huguenots among them. While Jewish settlers were few in numbers, they played a significant role in business and included the first two mayors of Auckland and the colonial premier, Sir Julius Vogel. Smaller groups such as the Baptists, Congregationalists, Society of Friends and Salvation Army had a visible presence.

As old-world arrangements for structuring society faced new-world sociological patterns, religious pluralism came to challenge denominational identity. For Anglicans with their numerical superiority and tradition of an interdependence of church and state it was not always easy to think in terms of the new social realities. George Augustus Selwyn, who was "Bishop of New Zealand", gave the Anglicans leadership in adapting church institutions to the colonial environment. Appointed by the British crown and with half his salary paid by the Colonial Office, Selwyn initially found it difficult to distance himself from the state. New Zealand politicians, when they were asked in 1855 to pay for part of his salary, refused because it was seen as "departing from the principle of perfect civil equality of all the religious denominations".[6] Achieving this principle was not without difficulty. This was seen, for example, in the question of government subsidies to religious educational institutions and the licensing of ministers to conduct civil marriages.

Anglicans by their 1857 constitution established themselves by "voluntary compact" accepting "fundamental provisions" that acknowledged their English heritage. They developed a structure of synodical government with bishops, clergy and laity all contributing to the government of the church. The involvement of laymen (women at this stage were excluded) was an innovative move and in part reflected the way in which the church in a colonial society depended on lay support for its existence. At the same time Selwyn affirmed their links to their "mother church" and their desire to remain "faithful children". Adaptation was the fruit of necessity as the church restructured itself to undertake its mission in the colonial context. But given their English history and size, Anglicans could often act consciously or unconsciously as a quasi-established church, taking for example a prominent role in conducting religious services on civil occasions.

The process of adaptation to the colonial context can also be illustrated by the way in which Presbyterians largely avoided reproducing the divisions of Scotland. Ministers and people from the different Presbyterian bodies joined to form congregations and presbyteries that were brought together in 1862 in the Presbyterian Church of New Zealand. Despite the desire to avoid rivalry in the face of pioneering demands, Presbyterians divided geographically into a northern and southern church. The Free Church ethos found expression in the Synod of Otago and Southland, which retained its independent identity until the union of the two churches in 1901.

The role of the church in a colonial society was defined in different ways by the various denominations according to the traditions which moulded them. One area of conflict in New Zealand was education. The church in Britain over the centuries made important contributions to education but access to it was restricted by denominational affiliation. In the 19th century debates were taking place over the role of the state in making education available to all. In New Zealand this issue came to a climax in 1877. It was finally agreed by the government that primary education should be free, secular and compulsory.

This so called "secular clause" resulted in what its opponents called "godless schools". Attempts to gain acceptance even for a daily Bible reading and prayer, with exemptions for those whose parents did not want them to attend, failed. While there was a small group influenced by secularist thinking who felt that religion should be excluded from schools, the majority were influenced by the pressures of sectarianism. The inability of the churches to agree among themselves on the content of religious education, given New Zealand's pluralistic society, led politicians to adopt the secular clause.

In response Roman Catholics developed their own education system. They resented what they saw as double taxation — paying for the education of other people's children as well as their own — and the unwillingness of the government to subsidize their schools. Protestants put a great deal of energy into trying to have some form of religious education accepted into the school programme. In attempting this they developed voluntary alternatives outside school hours, along with Sunday schools and Bible classes for young people. Private church schools were developed at the secondary level. These were often accused of being elitist and available only to a small proportion of children.

As a result of denominational pluralism and the educational system, the gospel was very fragmented in 19th-century New Zealand. It was heard in voices with English, Irish, Scots and other accents and reflected the cultures from which people came. At worst these divisions resulted in bitter interdenominational rivalry inflamed by old-world religious prejudices and imported disputes. The majority of Roman Catholics originated from Ireland, and the Protestant-Catholic divide was reinforced by debates over Irish independence. The activities of the Protestant Political Association, led by a Baptist minister, which reached their peak during and immediately after the first world war, fanned the flames of anti-Catholic bigotry and for a few years infused New Zealand politics with unseemly religious altercations. At the family and community level intermarriage between Roman Catholics and Protestants was seen as a betrayal of one's own group. In spite of these divisions there were examples of cooperation across the Protestant-Catholic divide, particularly in rural communities.

While nearly 90 percent of the population identified themselves with one of the four major denominations in the 19th century, this did not translate into active church membership and participation. Less than 30 percent of the people attended church services. Colonial clergy frequently complained about the religious apathy and indifference among the majority. Attempts at evangelism by visiting preachers encouraged local congregations but seldom translated into permanent increases in membership. While people wanted access to the church for baptism, weddings and funerals, the majority were not found regularly within its walls. The gospel accepted by most people was therefore a limited one.

Protestant churches attempted to impose on society their moral agenda and in this they had some success. Sunday was seen as a day of rest and the well-being of society dependent on faithful obedience to the ten commandments. This approach resulted in negative proscriptions against what were seen as vices such as drunkenness, gambling and prostitution. At best it could translate into thriftiness, a concern for duty, loyalty, reliability, trustworthiness, hard work and enterprise. At worst it could turn into judgmental self-righteousness.

This found expression in the prohibition movement towards the end of the 19th and the beginning of the 20th century. Drunkenness and destitution were serious problems in colonial societies. The remedy of trying to outlaw all alcohol, while coming very close to achieving success, was resented by many as an attempt to impose puritanical constraints on the whole community. In the same way, attempts to place restrictions on gambling, a favourite colonial pastime, often reinforced divisions between church members and non-members.

The 19th century saw the emergence of a rapidly developing gulf between church members and the working class. The origin of this lay in Britain and it was transplanted on the migrant ships. Many colonists lost regular connection with the church before they left their place of origin. The imposition of moral standards on the community was seen by one commentator in 1899 as coercive and an attempt to promote "artificial righteousness". He concluded: "If your theology was as good as some of the liquor dispensed in our pubs the people would think more of the church." The denominations with their "different doctrines" were seen as "a gigantic fraud" with the majority of their ministers working "for gold and not for souls".[7]

Churches, while claiming to have a gospel for the whole of society, were in fact identified with subcultures which were often defined by historical, social and economic rather than theological or religious factors. The achievements of the churches in a colonial society were considerable and should not be underestimated. The extension of ministry throughout the whole country required, particularly in the early years, courage and strength in the face of privations and pioneering conditions. The support of ministry and the building of churches, ministers' residences and schools often required great financial sacrifices from those committed to the church. By the end of the 19th century, in the space of sixty years, churches were well organized with some noteworthy buildings and solid achievements in extending their ministry. Many examples could be given of outstanding ministers and lay leaders. But the Christianity brought to New Zealand in the 19th century in its migrant settler forms, not surprisingly, reflected a heavy dependence on old-world models of ministry, ways of worship, styles of architecture and leadership. While the churches engaged in some significant charitable work, they seem to have been preoccupied with a gospel which emphasized maintaining public order and moral respectability.

NOTES

[1] *The Home and Foreign Missionary Record for the Church of Scotland*, November 1841, p.404.
[2] *Ibid.*, July 1843, p.259.
[3] A. Newman, "A Study of the Causes Leading to the Extinction of the Maori", in *Transactions and the Proceedings of the New Zealand Institute*, Vol.14, 1881, p.477.
[4] Charlotte Godley, *Letters from Early New Zealand*, p.82.
[5] A.H. McLintock, *The History of Otago*, Dunedin, Otago Centennial Publications, 1949, p.192.
[6] Davidson and Lineham, *Transplanted Christianity*, p.88.
[7] *Ibid.*, p.232.

3. 1893: Reshaping Church and Society

HAIL SISTER ELECTORS!
September 19, 1893, divided the ages. A new era has dawned. We are in the year One of the Revolution.
> 'Peace hath her victories
> No less renowned than war.'

It was not good that the political man should be alone. Too long has he complacently offered his feet to be measured for his wife's shoes. Henceforth there will be more feet to measure, and fewer corns and blisters to endure.

This great reform — there has never been a greater — is not a gift or a concession to women. It is the yielding of a natural right long withheld and usurped. The right to make laws and the right of self-protection are one. The former grows out of the latter. Self-protection is the root; legislation is the tree. These rights are inalienable in men. They are also inalienable in women, for they need protection, not only in common with men, but sometimes against men. We are convinced that men, by ceasing to count themselves a whole when they are only a part, will not only do an act of justice to half the race, but will confer a boon upon themselves.[1]

A third defining moment in the history of Aotearoa New Zealand was the decision by the New Zealand legislature on 18 September 1893 to given women the vote. New Zealand became the first country in the world with universal suffrage for both women and men. The victory, celebrated in the quotation above from an editorial in *The New Zealand Methodist*, was seen as bringing in a new age in which women and men would share political equality.

The victory was in large measure achieved by the work of the Women's Christian Temperance Union (WCTU). Motivated by strong Christian ideals about the need to protect women and children from the evil impact of alcohol on them and society as a whole, members of the WCTU campaigned to gain the vote for women. They wanted to be able to bring electoral pressure to bear on members of parliament so that legislation controlling and even prohibiting the manufacture, sale and distribution of alcohol could be enacted. The WCTU was more than a single-issue organization, placing its opposition to alcohol within its "Crusade for Social Purity".

Churches were divided on the need for prohibition. Those aligned with a more evangelical stance — Baptists, Methodists and the Salvation Army — identified with the campaign. Most Presbyterians supported prohibition, while many Anglicans, and even more Roman Catholics, were opposed to it. The churches and their leaders were also divided on the question of extending suffrage to women. In 1892 the editor of *The New Zealand Presbyterian* concluded that "female franchise would improve neither the condition of women nor the character of our colonial politics".[2]

Women in 19th-century colonial society were often described as "helpmeets". Their role was defined by their husband's work and the cultural expectations sanctified by tradition. The church reinforced these values, unconsciously by its patriarchal structure and consciously by its theological teaching about the status of women. Women were seen as the supporters, if not servants, of their husbands. That was quite clearly the case for the wives of the missionaries, although in many cases they acted as missionaries in their own right. While some of the husbands, for example Henry Williams, saw their wives as "fellow helpers", the demands of domesticity and rearing of children put constraints on women that men did not suffer.

In the early years men significantly outnumbered women in Pakeha society. In 1858 there were 130.6 males per 100 females; in 1901 the ratio was still 111:100. Single women were encouraged to migrate from Britain to correct this imbalance. Little account has been taken of the impact of this gender disparity on the colonial church, although the complaints of ministers in the early pioneering years about indifference and apathy possibly reflected this. Social historians have pointed to social problems such as drunkenness and violence being an outcome of the male world. The prohibition movement was a response to these social problems and their impact on women in particular.

The role of the colonial "helpmeet" was based on the values of home and family. The majority of Christian women who campaigned for the vote were domestic rather than radical feminists. They wanted to maintain and safeguard values associated with the family rather than bring about a radical reconstruction of gender roles. There were however some notable exceptions, such as Kate Sheppard and Christina Henderson, both active church women, who campaigned for social, political and financial equality between women and men.

Well into the 20th century the churches sanctified domesticity and motherhood as almost the only vocation open to women. Within the churches women's organizations became important in reinforcing this. The Mothers' Union, which began in the Anglican Church in New Zealand in 1886, was an extension of the organization founded in England. The Christchurch Mothers' Union declared in 1894 that its objective was "to awaken in all mothers a sense of their great responsibility as mothers in the training of their boys and girls who will be the future fathers and mothers of New Zealand; and to organize in every place a band of mothers who will unite in prayer, and seek by their own example to lead their families in purity and holiness".[3]

The women's organizations were controlled by women and became the sphere of church life which was exclusively theirs. Through them women became actively involved in voluntary charitable work among the poor and disadvantaged and in supporting overseas missions. Their significant contributions in these areas should not be underestimated. Women were not encouraged to have careers outside the home but to raise their own families and take part in church activities.

A social barrier developed between "church women" and those who were forced by economic adversity and often social status to take up work. This reinforced both the divide between the church and the largely non-churchgoing working class and the identification of the church with middle-class society and values.

Within the Roman Catholic Church religious orders provided a recognized vocation for women. Most of the sisters who came to New Zealand were brought to teach in the burgeoning alternative Catholic education system. The majority of these sisters were from Ireland and through their role in the classroom they reinforced the strong Irish flavour of the church. Outstanding among the Catholic religious was Mother Mary-Joseph Aubert. A French woman, she initially taught both Maori and Pakeha children in Auckland. After twelve years working in Hawke's Bay as district nurse among Maori, she moved in 1883 to Jerusalem on the Wanganui River. There she ran a school and undertook medical work. In 1892 she set up the first indigenous order in New Zealand, the Daughters of Our Lady of Compassion, and in 1899 she extended her work to Wellington. Her sisters became involved in caring for poor invalids and orphans and providing a soup kitchen and day nursery. In other denominations deaconess orders also became involved in social work which often directed ministry to the urban poor and rural Maori.

The voice of the church, which as we have seen was largely silent over the alienation of Maori land, was seldom raised when other issues of community concern were noted. In 1888 Rutherford Waddell, a Presbyterian minister in Dunedin, drew attention in a sermon to the exploitation of women seamstresses who were being paid what he called "starvation wages" for piece-work. At a meeting of the Presbyterian Synod of Otago and Southland he called on ministers to "proclaim more emphatically the laws of Christ, as laws of commercial and social, as well as religious life".[4] But the synod decided that "it was rather out of the province of the church's special work", and "while expressing deep sympathy with the victims of the system" only passed "a general resolution".[5]

At a subsequent public meeting Waddell pointed out that respectable church members were involved in the firms exploiting women workers. He was instrumental in bargaining with employers and in organizing a Tailoresses' Union, serving as its first president. Waddell was also appointed to a government Royal Commission set up to investigate the complaints. His action, however, was exceptional as far as the churches were concerned. They were happy to undertake charitable work among orphans and those who fell on hard times, but they were not willing to address underlying social and economic root causes.

The churches attempted to give expression to Jesus' teaching about loving one's neighbour, but tended to approach issues of welfare and social change from an individualistic perspective. The regeneration of society for them depended on the conversion of the individual and the rooting out of moral evil. The gospel they preached was therefore aimed at bringing about transformation of individuals rather than of society at large. Apart from their special moral campaigns and their concerns over Sunday observance and religious education in schools, the churches largely avoided involvement in the political process. While the churches thought of New Zealand as a Christian nation, sectarianism discouraged the emergence of a national sense of Christian identity and the churches' apolitical approach encouraged a privatized spirituality.

The achievement of universal suffrage, therefore, while a significant moment in the history of Aotearoa New Zealand in itself, did not bring the new era which some campaigners expected. Discrimination on the grounds of gender was extensive in the 1890s in New Zealand and was reinforced by cultural assumptions. At the political level women were not eligible to stand for parliament until 1919, and the first woman was not elected until 1933. In 1993, when the country marked the centennial of suffrage, it was noted that over the one hundred years only 36 women, in contrast to well over 1000 men, had been members of parliament. The journey towards equality has been a long one and in many areas is still incomplete.

The churches were slow in making room for women within their institutional life, although they were usually in advance of the churches in the countries from which they had come. Anglican women were given the right to vote at church meetings only in 1919 and could not take part in all the councils of the church until 1922. But not until 1972 did the first women members appear in the general synod, the highest body of the church. Presbyterians first allowed women to become elders — and thereby attend session, presbytery and general assembly meetings — in 1955. Methodist, Baptist and Congregational churches, in contrast, all had women attending their national meetings by the early years of this century.

The Salvation Army was exceptional in giving leadership to women, one woman noting in 1892 that "the Army has broken down the orthodox belief that woman's place is at home, and has given us what has long been needed — unrestrained liberty of action and thought".[6] The first Congregational woman minister arrived in New Zealand from Scotland in 1951. The first Methodist woman minister was ordained in 1959, followed by a Presbyterian in 1965, a Baptist in 1973 and Anglicans in 1977. Methodist, Presbyterian and Anglican churches now have significant numbers of women ministers. They have served as president of the Methodist conference and moderator of the Presbyterian general assembly, and the first Anglican woman diocesan bishop in the world was ordained in Dunedin in 1990.

One commentator, writing 25 years after the ordination of the first Presbyterian woman minister, noted that "although the structures have changed to allow women into ministry, the church (ordained and lay) attitude to who women are and what they can do has not changed to the same extent. Discrimination because of sex is still a matter for debate, and women's equality is still open to question."[7] Moreover, the willingness of the church to open itself to the challenges of women's perspectives and feminist theology is a more fundamental challenge.

The shifts in the role of women in the church were often preceded by the changes taking place in the wider society. This was seen, for example, in the Government Service Equal Pay Act in 1960 which provided parity for men and women doing comparable work, the broadening of career opportunities for women and the introduction of legislation guaranteeing freedom from discrimination on the grounds of gender. One may therefore ask to what extent changes in New Zealand culture have been directly related to the gospel and to what extent they have resulted from social and political forces. The changes in the church have been both supported and opposed by theological arguments largely dependent on the global debates. That was demonstrated in the organized opposition by conservative church women and the contrasting support by other women for the United Nations Convention on the Elimination of All Forms of Discrimination Against Women, which was ratified by the government in 1984.

Throughout the 20th century and particularly since the 1960s there have been rapid shifts in many of the cultural norms in New Zealand society. This is seen, for example, in the institutions of marriage and family and changing attitudes towards divorce. For much of the 20th century in families with children the mother was a full-time homemaker. By 1995 both parents in the majority of two-parent families had paid jobs outside the home and one-quarter of all families had a solo parent. Cohabitation has increasingly been accepted in preference to marriage. In 1993, 38 percent of all births were outside of wedlock, compared with 9 percent in 1963. With the exception of Roman Catholics most churches have gradually accepted divorce as a social necessity and the remarriage of divorcees within the church as ecclesiastically acceptable.

Social changes have been accompanied by profound shifts in New Zealand's economic policies. The 19th-century laissez-faire philosophy, which exalted the virtues of individualism, reinforced pioneering success. In the 1890s New

Zealand began a shift towards state intervention in the promotion of social well-being. This was seen in the provision of old-age pensions, the break-up of large estates and the redistribution of land, and the settlement of industrial disputes by arbitration. Politicians were motivated by a combination of pragmatism, progressive ideas and Fabian philosophy with little indication of any direct Christian input. New Zealand promoted the image of an egalitarian society in which everyone had equal opportunity.

The shift towards a social welfare state came after the election of a Labour government in 1935. The Depression following the Wall Street crash in 1929, resulting in high unemployment, reduction in wages and inability to pay mortgages, contributed to widespread community and individual distress. The churches, particularly through their city missions, made compassionate and in some cases creative responses to the enormous need. They became increasingly aware that their pious platitudes and prayers for national regeneration failed to remedy the national economic woes and social damage.

Some politicians, motivated by Christian ideals, joined with other socialists in shaping the Labour Party's philosophy. This was seen by them as the political embodiment of the Golden Rule and the parable of the good Samaritan. The social welfare system instituted by the first Labour government aimed to provide cradle-to-the-grave care for everyone through universal health care, state housing for those who could not provide their own, a wide range of subsidized public services and free education through to the tertiary level. It is impossible to quantify the Christian influence on the development of the social welfare state. Until the emergence of the Christian Heritage Party and the Christian Democrats in the 1990s, with the overt identification of their own particular view of fundamentalist Christianity with their political organizations, Christianity was largely expressed in New Zealand politics through particular issues and campaigns.

The welfare state itself became part of the New Zealand social structure, accepted by all political parties. Its dismemberment, first under the fourth Labour government in the 1980s and then under its successor National government in the 1990s, resulted from the implementation of monetarist policies with their emphasis on "user pays" and the downscaling of government support, and the privatization of public services. Great pressure has been placed on the health and education systems in the pursuit of efficiency.

The egalitarian society, which always had some mythic dimensions, has been replaced by a reassertion of laissez-faire individualism. The sad result has been a society in which the divisions between rich and poor have rapidly increased. While many have achieved material prosperity and benefited financially, the social costs of economic restructuring have been widespread. The government continues to provide considerable social assistance through benefits to the socially disadvantaged, but many families now rely on food parcels to supplement their income.

The churches have been at the forefront of those attempting to meet the needs of the victims of social changes. They have also taken a lead in representing to government the human costs of its policies. In 1993 church leaders issued a Social Justice Statement which promoted the welfare of the whole community. They entered into dialogue with politicians and encouraged the study of social justice issues within churches.

The relationship between gospel and culture is challenged by the social changes New Zealand has experienced. The church, in extolling the virtues of family and identifying with a particular cultural expression of this, has been slow in adapting to the new social realities. There are some who would say that the church should maintain its standards irrespective of what is happening in society at large. The more fundamental question about what the gospel teaches concerning family values needs deeper investigation. The church has too easily been locked into defending inherited social institutions which reflect historical and cultural forces that are not necessarily representative of gospel values. At the same time there is a danger if the church allows its values to be determined by the latest social trend.

The denominations that came to New Zealand have often reacted to social change rather than led it. The message of the church was often heard most loudly through its negative preaching, no to divorce, no to alcohol, no to gambling, no to recreational activities on Sunday. The positive dimensions of its gospel, loving one's neighbour, expressed in its social service work, were often too easily taken for granted.

The churches' reaction to the economic changes of the 1980s and 1990s indicated that for some church members the gospel was seen to have a direct bearing on the way in which society dealt particularly with the disadvantaged and marginalized. But churches have difficulty sustaining prophetic initiatives over a long period, and it usually falls to individuals and small groups to maintain prophetic vigilance. Other groups, who also claim to represent gospel values, have taken diametrically opposite positions supporting (for example) monetarist policies and individualism. The gospel as a result has been heard coming from different positions, resulting in confusion, with politicians often listening to the voices which serve their own interests.

NOTES

[1] *The New Zealand Methodist*, 23 September 1893.
[2] *The New Zealand Presbyterian*, 1 October 1892, p.71.
[3] B. Archer, *A History of the Mothers' Union and the Association of Anglican Women in New Zealand*, p.3.
[4] *Proceedings of the Synod of Otago and Southland*, 1888, p.29.
[5] *The New Zealand Presbyterian*, 1 December 1888, p.109.
[6] C.R. Bradwell, *Fight the Good Fight: The Story of the Salvation Army in New Zealand 1883-1983*, Wellington, Reed, 1982, p.123.
[7] Vivienne Adair, *Women of the Burning Bush*, Wellington, Presbyterian Church of New Zealand, 1991, p.6.

4. 1940: God's Own Country

> The Conference of the Methodist Church of New Zealand, now in annual session, realizes and accepts the responsibility of expressing its mind about ethical aspects of the present international crisis. The constraint to do so arises ... from its solemn sense of accountability to God for its every corporate utterance, especially at so critical a time...
>
> The Conference hereby records its distress at the outbreak of war, its abhorrence of deeds betokening a pagan and brutal disregard of human rights and its longing for a just and lasting peace. It attests also to its eagerness that the church it represents should serve to the utmost the worthy purpose of bringing about this peace...
>
> The Conference registers its belief that the British Empire, while far from perfect, has pre-eminently served the growth of free institutions in the world, and that it remains an indispensable unit in the defences of these essentially Christian elements in any adequately good social fabric...
>
> The Conference declares its loyalty to the British Crown and Commonwealth, gives thanks for the Christian life and example of Their Majesties our King and Queen and is grateful that British statesmanship in all political parties, after arduous endeavours to maintain international peace, is united in taking the only honourable course left.[1]

New Zealand's involvements in the first and second world wars were significant defining moments for the identity of the country and its people. The quotation above comes from a "Statement on Peace and War" issued by the Methodist conference in 1940. Other churches passed similar resolutions regretting the war, acknowledging the failure of the churches to prevent it and reluctantly, but with a strong sense of necessity, committing themselves to taking part in it. The evolution of New Zealand's identity as a country was closely related to its involvement in overseas wars.

In the 19th century New Zealand was often defined in terms of its indigenous inhabitants as "Maoriland". For people coming from different parts of Britain and Europe national unity was only slowly forged. The rugged geography of the country, its isolation and lack of transport, along with patterns of settlement, contributed to parochialism. The semi-federal structure established in 1852, with a national parliament and provincial governments, encouraged national versus regional tensions. The provinces were abolished in 1876 but local loyalties remained strong.

The churches only slowly developed their national structures, and for most Christians denominational identity was defined by membership at a parish or congregational level. Four varieties of British Methodism came to New Zealand in the last century. Three of these — Wesleyan, United Free and Bible Christian Methodists — united in 1896. The Primitive Methodists joined the Methodist Church of New Zealand in 1913 and in the same year the church gained its autonomy by separating from the Australasian general conference. We have already noted that Presbyterians were divided geographically until the union of the southern and northern churches in 1901. The 1857 Anglican constitution resulted in a church in which the dioceses had more influence on the local parish than the general synod. Catholic identity was also shaped by its diocesan structure and its links with Rome. Smaller churches like the Baptists and Congregationalists came together in national unions in 1882 and 1884 respectively, but their polity placed power in the local unit rather than the national body. Presbyterians and Methodists through their annual assembly and conference and their committee structures were the most effective of the churches in dealing with national issues.

The evolution of New Zealand identity was encouraged by the growth of myth-making. Thomas Bracken, the author of New Zealand's national anthem, "God Defend New Zealand", eulogized the country in 1890 in another poem he called "God's Own Country":

> Give me, give me God's own country! there to live and there to die.
> God's own country! fairest region resting 'neath the southern sky,

> God's own country! framed by Nature in her grandest, noblest mould;
> Land of peace and land of plenty, land of wool and corn and gold.[2]

The myth-makers extolled the country's rugged beauty, its political freedom, the leadership it gave to women's suffrage and other social welfare legislation in the 1890s, and its abundance and plenty. There was an element of jingoism in this picture which took no account of such things as the unjust alienation of Maori land, the deleterious impact of Pakeha on the Maori population and the racist attitudes promoted by the government towards non-Europeans, exemplified in its selective immigration policy.

This rhetoric was accompanied by an idealization of the motherland, which for most migrants was Britain. For a significant minority, mainly Roman Catholics, Ireland, rather than England, Wales or Scotland was "home". Loyalty to New Zealand and to the motherland came together in a patriotic fervour towards the British empire which in its extreme form could become quite xenophobic.

This was seen in New Zealand's support at the turn of the century for the imperial cause during the Anglo-Boer war in South Africa and the largely uncritical support of the churches. In 1900, for example, the Methodist conference passed a "Patriotic Motion" in which they rejoiced "'in the patriotic feeling' expressed in the country and 'the heroism shown by her contingents, and the liberal response of the colony to the appeal for funds'. They prayed 'that the complete and decisive victory of our forces may soon end the bloodshed' and were thankful for 'the intense loyalty to the throne and the closer union of all parts of the Empire'."[3] Critics of the war like the member of parliament T.E. Taylor and the Presbyterian minister Rutherford Waddell tended to be lone voices, overwhelmed by the patriotic fervour of both the country and the churches.

The uncritical linking of God, king and country came together particularly during the first world war. New Zealand made a notable contribution to the Allied cause. It had one of the highest per capita casualty rates among the combatants: one in seventeen New Zealanders were either killed or injured in the conflict. The most famous engagement was at Gallipoli in Turkey, where Australian and New Zealand forces landed on 25 April 1915. Despite their retreat, the Anzacs (from "Australian and New Zealand Army Corp") gained a reputation for bravery under fire and courage in the face of insurmountable odds. In 1920, 25 April was fixed as Anzac day, and it was "treated as a holy day, as Sunday".[4] Its annual observance became an act of civil religion, extolling the virtues of patriotism, loyalty, imperialism and the sanctifying of the dead. Churches identified themselves with this, with ministers leading in prayers and hymns at both civil and religious Anzac day services.

Most New Zealand Christians, with the exception of groups like the Brethren, Seventh-day Adventists and the Society of Friends, uncritically supported the war effort. The mainline churches supplied chaplains to the forces. Their ministry was restricted by denominational divisions and resented by many soldiers who disliked compulsory attendance at church parades. The war highlighted the growing gulf between men and the church and reinforced a strong sense of disillusionment many had about the message of Christianity. In supporting the Allied cause church leaders were faced with trying to justify the mounting casualty lists. The language used by the church, sanctifying the death of soldiers in sacrificial language, did not make sense of the carnage, the waste of human life and individual suffering. For the ordinary soldier, mateship or a spirit of brotherhood with his friends broke down denominational barriers. Fatalism in the face of imminent death was more important for many than faith in God.

Dissent expressed against the war was harshly dealt with by the New Zealand authorities. The country adopted conscription, which was endorsed by most church leaders. One chaplain told Methodist young men that "they were morally obliged to fight the shirker... to the last trench".[5] New Zealand had one of the most stringent policies regarding conscientious objection among the Allies, although as the war progressed, some church leaders called for greater sympathy towards "genuine" objectors.

The first world war had a profound impact on New Zealand society. As a small country very few families were untouched by the conflict. The lists of casualties on the large honours boards erected in churches and the civic war memorials are reminders of the extent of this suffering. Resolutions passed by churches at the end of the war reflected "a sense of war weariness, profound thanksgiving that it had ended, pride in victory, sorrow at the sadness and injury caused and a strong desire for peace".[6]

The churches performed significant pastoral ministry among the grieving, but in their identification with the rhetoric associated with the war they unconsciously helped make it possible. The leading Presbyterian minister, James Gibb, confessed, "I was as good as a recruiting agent during the war."[7] He became an active pacifist, supporting the League of Nations and working to bring churches together on the issues of national disarmament and the renunciation of war. This idealism encouraged a growing minority, notably among Methodist young people, to identify themselves as pacifists. The Methodist minister Ormond Burton, a highly decorated soldier who became a pacifist, took a leading part in forming the Christian Pacifist Society in 1935.

The gospel heard from most of the churches during the first world war echoed and supported the secular sentiments in favour of the Allied cause. The outbreak of war in 1939 came as a challenge to the churches. They avoided the jingoism of 1914 and expressed the need to support the war effort with measured resignation. Chaplains were much more effective than in the first world war. Protestant chaplains avoided denominational divisions and were attached to units, enabling them to be in closer touch with the soldiers. As a country New Zealand still had a very illiberal attitude towards dissent, although some church leaders attempted to modify this. Ormond Burton's absolute commitment to pacifism led to his dismissal from the Methodist ministry in 1942. He, like many Christian pacifists, faced fines and imprisonment and the suspension of his civil rights.

During the first world war Maori were divided over the kind of support they should give to the war effort. Waikato Maori under the leadership of Te Puea Herangi resisted conscription, seeing the conflict as a Pakeha issue. Those Maori who served in Europe were often treated as second-class soldiers. Maori made a considerable contribution to the New Zealand effort in the second world war through their own battalion, which suffered severe losses. Among those who survived were men who gave notable leadership to the fight to preserve Maori culture, language and identity. But the recognition of Maori equality during the war was not translated into economic and social benefits for Maori after it.

New Zealand's sense of nationhood was forged as people joined together in a common cause which transcended regional, ethnic and religious differences. Pakeha New Zealanders, while tracing their origins to Britain and Europe, became more aware of their distinctive identity. They were not British but Kiwis, New Zealanders, Diggers or Anzacs.[8] The Asian and Pacific conflict during the second world war reinforced New Zealand's sense of geographical location in the southwest Pacific. The war came very close to home, and it was the US forces which stemmed the Japanese southward tide.

Psychologically many New Zealanders after the second world war still continued to think of Britain as "home". This was reinforced by continuing migration from Europe and the heavy reliance of New Zealand on British markets for the sale of its agricultural exports. This changed with Britain's entry into the European Community. By the 1970s New Zealand was aware that its economic and political destiny was not as an outpost of the British Empire but as a nation in the Asia-Pacific region.

Until the 1960s the identity of the churches was largely shaped by their northern hemisphere roots. Anglicans often drew their leadership from the Church of England. All churches were influenced by the Anglo-European theological tradition. While New Zealand produced some competent theologians there was still a very heavy dependence on overseas thinking. The ecumenical movement in New Zealand reflected that. The breaking down of barriers between denominations was encouraged by such things as the Student Christian Movement, the International Missionary, Life and Work and Faith and Order conferences and the formation of the World Council of Churches. New Zealanders were inspired by these developments, the visits by ecumenical leaders — for example, John R. Mott in 1896, 1903 and 1926 — and participation in the overseas conferences.

There were local expressions of this rising ecumenical tide. Presbyterians and Methodists entered into union negotiations as early as 1902. These continued on and off for many years. They were joined by Congregationalists but were unable to overcome the opposition of minority groups. In 1955 the Churches of Christ joined in discussions with these three churches and in 1964 the Joint Commission on Church Union, which also included Anglicans, was formed. *The Plan for Union*, issued in 1971, envisaged the union of the five negotiating churches to form the Church of Christ in New Zealand. Success was nearly achieved but denominational separatism won the day. Cooperation between the churches, however, was enhanced at many levels.

The ecumenical movement helped to overcome the sectarian spirit which was part of the legacy of colonial Christianity. The formation of the National Council of Churches (NCC) in 1941 brought together the Protestant churches to work together on ecumenical endeavours. One of its first actions was to organize the Campaign for Christian Order. The churches tried to bring Christian principles to bear on the shaping of society in order to prepare for post-war reconstruction. There was an underlying desire to develop New

Zealand as a Christian society. While much was gained from the ecumenical cooperation, it was questionable whether New Zealand religious life was "appreciably different because of the activities of the Campaign".[9]

The NCC became an important ecumenical midwife promoting interdenominational cooperation. The Second Vatican Council (1963-65) opened new relationships between Protestants and Catholics. The Joint NCC and Roman Catholic Church Working Committee, which met between 1969 and 1984, helped to break down barriers and build up trust. The formation in 1988 of the Conference of Churches in Aotearoa New Zealand brought Roman Catholics into membership of the ecumenical body which replaced the NCC. The Baptists, however, decided not to join the new organization. The ecumenical tide, which reached its peak in the 1950s and 1960s, had waned with the reassertion of denominational identity and new theological alliances across denominational boundaries.

Attempts to promote church union and the growth of ecumenical cooperation were national expressions of a worldwide trend which sought to express Christian identity through new patterns of relationships. But the churches failed to develop a distinctive New Zealand Christian ethos. While the churches increasingly cooperated with one another, there were clear indications that they were struggling to maintain their place in society.

Throughout the 20th century there has been a general decline in the number of people identifying with the church. Since the mid-1960s in particular, the major churches have suffered from the dramatic erosion of their membership, indicated by the five-yearly national census returns. Anglicans declined from 33.7 percent of the population in 1966 to 22.1 percent in 1991, Presbyterians from 21.8 to 16.3 percent, and Methodists from 7.0 to 4.2 percent. Roman Catholics in the same period have declined more slowly, from 15.9 to 15.0 percent. Large increases have been seen in the number who declare "no religion", from 1.2 to 20.1

percent. The major churches have a declining, ageing membership while smaller churches such as the Baptists, Assemblies of God and other Pentecostal groups, have shown signs of growth and a younger age profile.

The factors underlying these changes are complex. Some have pointed to the impact of secularization with its roots in the Enlightenment. New Zealand developed as a country in which religious values, beliefs and rituals were seen increasingly as belonging to the private sphere rather than to society as a whole. The Christendom model with its close relationship between church and state which some of the denominations embraced was only fitfully employed in New Zealand. No one church had establishment status, although Anglicans often acted as de facto chaplain to the nation. The experiences of the churches during the first world war indicated that in providing a sacred canopy for the war effort they identified too closely with the military cause and were not able to distance themselves from its tragic outcome.

The churches often claimed a special status, as of right, that was difficult to defend as secular values became more prevalent. The defence of sabbatarianism and prohibition were examples. People increasingly questioned the right of the church to impose its moral or social agenda on the whole society. Religious pluralism in the 19th century gave rise to denominational sectarianism. In the 20th century the growth of toleration and religious pluralism resulted in greater secularization and the marginalization of the churches. Secular celebrants for weddings and funerals now offer alternative possibilities to what traditionally was the monopoly of the church. The churches no longer have the right to free time on national radio or television. Christian festivals such as Easter and Christmas have been commercialized in ways that bear little contact with the underlying religious meaning of these celebrations.

Churchgoing was once associated with social respectability, and the baptism of children and marriage in a church were considered as necessary rites of passage. Increased leisure activities, mobility and prosperity have meant that people have a variety of choices about how they spend their weekends. Many now get along quite well without the church, which is seen as a voluntary society akin to a hobby or leisure activity, rather than as a place which deals with questions of ultimate significance. Churches have joined the many voices contending for a hearing in the pluralistic society which developed in New Zealand.

In the late 20th century, New Zealand expresses its identity through such things as its preoccupation with sport. The winning of the America's Cup in yachting in 1995 brought the whole country together in an outburst of national pride and expressions of patriotism. The activities of the All Blacks, the New Zealand rugby team, have much more impact on national identity than any religious activity. Sporting heroes are given the status of minor gods and sporting occasions become almost secular religious occasions. The definition of national identity in terms of war and sport, however, is a very male interpretation. Feminist critiques would rightly point to the need to examine the contribution that women have made to the shaping of New Zealand society both within and beyond the dominant patriarchal forces.

At the end of the 20th century New Zealand identified itself as a nuclear-free country, opposed to the testing, proliferation and transportation of nuclear weapons. This was not without some cost in international circles, with the sabotage of a Greenpeace vessel in Auckland harbour by French government agents in 1985 and the loss of defence and economic privileges with the United States. The wholehearted support for the nuclear-free policy achieved by the 1990s represented a remarkable development.

Among the significant contributors to this were activists motivated by Christian concern for the well-being of the world and its peoples. George Armstrong, an Anglican priest and theological teacher, founded the Peace Squadron in 1975 to blockade Auckland harbour against the visit of nuclear warships, and encouraged the nuclear-free movement. There was a symbolic David and Goliath dimension to this protest, with the small yachts and canoes of the protesters confronting warships that would neither confirm nor deny that they were carrying nuclear weapons. Church statements and studies promoted the nuclear-free policy which contributed to the groundswell of community support, which emboldened the Labour Government in the 1980s to pass legislation banning the visit of nuclear-powered or -armed ships. The growth of anti-nuclear opposition was seen in the way the vast majority of the community and politicians opposed French nuclear testing at Muroroa in 1995 and 1996.

Until the mid-1960s New Zealand thought of itself as a Christian nation, and the churches often acted as though they were the sole preservers of Christian culture which they believed the whole country should embrace. Slowly and painfully churches have had to come to terms with their marginal status and the post-Christendom age in which they live. The example of the move to a nuclear-free country points to the way in which churches and Christians contribute from within their own world to the much larger society of which they are a part. Churches and Christians cannot presume to speak for the whole, but they have spoken effectively in ways which have contributed to the shaping of New Zealand identity and its culture and at some points brought the gospel to bear on its life.

NOTES

[1] Davidson and Lineham, *Transplanted Christianity*, pp.297-99.
[2] G. McLauchlan, *The Illustrated Encyclopedia of New Zealand*, Auckland, Bateman, 1986, p.483.
[3] A.K. Davidson, *Christianity in Aotearoa: A History of Church and Society in New Zealand*, Wellington, Education for Ministry, 1991, p.95.

[4] *Ibid.*, p.101.
[5] *Ibid.*, p.99.
[6] *Ibid.*, p.100.
[7] *Ibid.*
[8] The name "Kiwi" comes from the flightless bird which is distinctive to New Zealand. "Digger" has its origin in the first world war, describing the troops who dug trenches; it was also used to describe Australians.
[9] Davidson, *Christianity in Aotearoa*, p.121.

5. 1990: The Challenge of Cultures

I want to quote from Psalm 137:
"By the rivers of Babylon we sat down. There we wept when we remembered Zion."

It is much more expressive in Maori and I take liberties with scripture.

"*I te taha o nga wai o Waitangi noho ana tatou I reira. A, e tangi ana tatou kia tatou ka mahara kia Hiro.*" [By the waters of Waitangi we sat down. We cried when we remembered Zion.]

Some of us have come here to celebrate, some to commemorate, some to commiserate, but some to remember what happened on this sacred ground.

We come to this sacred ground because our *tupuna* (ancestors) left us this ground. A hundred and fifty years ago a compact was signed, a covenant was made between two people. To this place where a treaty was signed to give birth to a nation — a unique and unusual circumstance...

But since the signing of that treaty 150 years ago I want to remind our partners that you have marginalized us. You have not honoured the treaty. We have not honoured each other in the promises we made on this sacred ground...

And so I come to the waters of Waitangi to weep for what could have been a unique document in the history of the world of indigenous people against the Pakeha, and I still have the hope that we can do it. Let us sit and listen to one another.[1]

Whakahuihui Vercoe, the Anglican Bishop of Aotearoa, spoke these words on 6 February 1990 at the 150th anniversary commemorating the signing of the treaty of Waitangi. This sesquicentennial observance was a defining moment in the history of Aotearoa New Zealand as a Maori bishop, in the presence of Queen Elizabeth II, the governor general, the prime minister, overseas diplomatic representatives, politicians and dignitaries, people and protesters, reminded those present of both the promises and the failures that the treaty of Waitangi symbolized. Ironically, Bishop Vercoe chose his text from Psalm 137, the same one that John Macfarlane, the first resident Presbyterian minister in New Zealand, used in February 1840 in his first sermon in the country, to remind the early settlers to remain faithful to the faith of their fathers and mothers. Bishop Vercoe in calling to mind Maori ancestors pointed to the compact, the covenant which they signed in front of Captain Hobson, the representative of Queen Elizabeth's ancestor, Queen Victoria.

The commemoration at Waitangi in 1990 included a church service, an appropriate reminder of the significant role which the missionaries played in gaining Maori adherence to the treaty. Four Anglican bishops took part, including the former archbishop, Sir Paul Reeves, who was at the time governor general, and Bishop Takuira Mariu, a Maori Catholic bishop. Notably absent were representatives from other churches — in particular Methodists, who were present at Waitangi in 1840 and whose missionaries encouraged many Maori to sign the treaty. The absence of Methodists at the 1990 commemoration resulted from the boycott which they observed. This boycott, and the presence of a very vocal group of protestors shouting "Honour the treaty" during the service and speeches at Waitangi, were a reminder that, as Bishop Vercoe indicated, the Pakeha partner had "not honoured the treaty" and that together Maori and Pakeha had "not honoured each other in the promises we made on this sacred ground".

Despite the belief of many Pakeha last century that Maori were a dying race and the view of at least some that they were being replaced by a superior people, Maori did not die out. The Maori population reached its lowest point in 1896 at 42,000 but by 1991 nearly 13 percent of the total population of the country — over 434,000 — were Maori.

The 19th century saw the sale, confiscation and alienation of the majority of Maori land as it passed into the hands of Pakeha settlers or the Crown. Deeply rooted grievances among Maori tribes over the loss of this land were not resolved by commissions and in some cases the payment of compensation. In the 1970s and 1980s public protests — for example in 1975 the *hikoi* (land march), which traversed the length of the North Island ending in the capital Wellington —

brought pressure on politicians to try to resolve the grievances. The setting up of the Waitangi Tribunal in 1975 and the granting to it in 1985 of powers to investigate land claims as far back as 1840, resulted in hearings which unearthed the often illegal and unjust ways in which land was transferred out of Maori hands. Some land since 1985 has been returned to Maori along with financial compensation, but many cases still remain to be resolved. Anglican and Methodist churches took a lead in examining how they acquired land. In some cases in which it was no longer used for the purpose for which it was given by Maori, it was returned to its traditional owners.

Maori as *tangata whenua* (people of the land) take their identity from the place in which their *tupuna* or ancestors lived. The alienation of land and the lack of an economic base to support the growing Maori population fostered Maori migration to urban areas after the second world war. Three-quarters of Maori lived in rural areas in 1945; by the mid-1970s three-quarters lived in urban areas. For many Maori this has been a dislocating process as they and their children lost touch with their place of origin. Many of the social indicators reflected in 1995 statistics confirmed how Maori are disadvantaged in their own land. They had higher infant mortality rates (13.1 compared with 6.2 per thousand), lower life expectancy (68 and 73 for Maori men and women; 73.1 and 78.9 for others), higher rates of imprisonment (43 percent of male prison inmates were Maori), and lower educational attainments than the rest of the community.[2]

Within Maori society important movements have contributed to the renaissance of their culture. In the 1890s the Young Maori Party grew out of Te Aute College, an Anglican boys' high school for Maori. The party included Apirana Ngata, who was the first Maori graduate (he graduated in both arts and law in the 1890s) and served as a member of parliament for 38 years. As a cabinet minister he encouraged both Maori agricultural and cultural development. He took a leading role as an Anglican Maori layman. Another member of the group, although not a Te Aute old boy, was Frederick Bennett, the first Bishop of Aotearoa.

While the churches slowly re-entered the Maori areas they left because of the wars of the 1860s, they did not easily regain the ground they lost. Maori movements had their own followings, bringing together political and religious concerns within a Maori cultural context. The rise of the Ratana Church, founded by T.W. Ratana after the first world war, also brought together religious and political aspirations. In 1925 the Anglican bishops of the North Island issued a pastoral letter excommunicating those who accepted Ratana's teaching. The census the following year indicated that nearly one-fifth of Maori identified themselves as Ratana.

As part of its response to the impact of Ratana, Anglicans decided to meet a long-felt need by giving Maori Anglicans their own bishop. Initially he was to have the same status as other diocesan bishops. When those making the appointment tried to appoint a Pakeha, the Maori response was "no Maori, no bishop". In 1928 a compromise resulted in the appointment of the Bishop of Aotearoa as a suffragan of the Bishop of Waiapu. He had no automatic seat on general synod and could attend only if elected as a diocesan clerical representative from Waiapu. He depended on the cooperation of diocesan bishops to allow him to exercise his episcopal ministry in their dioceses. This approval was not always forthcoming.

The Maori bishops brought their *mana* to the office, but they were handicapped institutionally in giving the kind of leadership needed by Maori. Gradually this position was remedied. In 1964 the bishop was given a full seat on general synod as a bishop. In 1978 *Te Pihopatanga o Aotearoa*, the Bishopric of Aotearoa, was given its own council. The bishop was licensed by the primate to undertake the oversight of Maori work throughout the country, although he still required permission from diocesan bishops to work in their dioceses. The general synod appointed a Bicultural Commission on the treaty of Waitangi in 1984. In its 1986 report it affirmed that the principles of partnership and bicultural development between Maori and Pakeha were found in the treaty of Waitangi. The church sought to give expression to these in its life. *Te Pihopatanga o Aotearoa* was put on the same basis as other diocesan bishops.

The constitution of the church, drawn up in 1857, was rewritten to give expression to the principles of partnership. This was approved in 1992 and made provision for three *tikanga* (ways): Maori, Pakeha and Polynesian (the Diocese of Polynesia covering mainly Fiji, Tonga and Samoa was given diocesan status in 1990). Each *tikanga* was given autonomy over its own respective area, but in areas of shared responsibility, particularly at the general synod level, the consent of the majority of each was required for measures to be approved.

In developing this system of structuring the ministry and government of the church, Anglicans sought to give institutional expression to the cultural realities of New Zealand history and life. While there was an attempt to assimilate Maori within the Pakeha structures, this was never effective. The new organization encouraged each *tikanga* to take responsibility for mission among its own people. For Maori that was seen in the division of Te Pihopatanga into five episcopal regions. They re-established their own theological college, Te Rau Kahikatea, sharing residential training with the College of the Southern Cross (the Pakeha college) at St John's College in Auckland. But Te Rau Kahikatea was also closely involved in the wider educational work of clergy and lay people throughout Te Pihopatanga.

The changes in the Anglican Church reflect an internal process within that institution as Anglicans have examined their history and their context and tried to shape their constitution in ways that affirm and give expression to cultural identity. Wider forces in society at large also encouraged these changes. Alongside the attention to Maori land grievances seen in the work of the Waitangi Tribunal there has been a renaissance of Maori culture. The founding of *Te Kohanga Reo* ("language nests"), where preschool Maori children have been immersed in *Te Reo Maori*, the Maori language, the recognition of Maori as an official language and the greater emphasis on its use and availability in schools and tertiary institutions have enabled many Maori and Pakeha to gain greater acquaintance with the language. Language is fundamental to the preservation and dynamic development of any culture. Within the Anglican Church, *The New Zealand Prayer Book — He Karakia Mihinare o Aotearoa*, published in 1989, brought together services in English and Maori.

Other churches have responded to the challenge of Maori identity in their own way and out of their own history. Methodists, for example, in contrast to Anglicans, did not reject T.W. Ratana and his movement. Attempts over many years to gain a separate synod for Maori work among Methodists, however, failed. In 1973 a Maori Division was inaugurated under R.D. Rakena as *Tumuaki* or head, which sought to realize "Maori styles of Christian life, witness and service, or a Maori response to the gospel..., reinforced by a wider recognition and appreciation all round that 'culture shapes the human voice that answers the voice of Christ'".[3] The Methodist conference in 1983 committed itself "to work towards the formation of a bicultural Methodist Church in Aotearoa as the essential first step on the journey towards multiculturalism".[4] This was given institutional expression by distinguishing Maori and *Tauiwi*, the other people or non-Maori. Both groups were given equal numbers on appointment committees and the council of the conference, and an equal voice in decision-making processes at the annual conference of the church.

When Captain Hobson greeted Maori after the signing of the treaty of Waitangi in 1840, he said to them, "*He iwi tahi tatou*" — we are now one people. The reality of New Zealand history is that the country has been made up of many peoples from different cultures. For much of its history since

1840 the country has sought either to assimilate or integrate Maori into Pakeha institutions and structures. This has also been the experience in the church. Some warn that the new structures carry with them the risk of separatism as groups based on ethnicity develop their life identified over against one another. The churches have attempted to emphasize the importance of partnership in the bicultural journey. This is not always easily achieved, but Maori as a minority group in their own land have often experienced the domination and alienation which the new arrangements seek to remedy.

Over three-quarters of the population in New Zealand trace their origins to Europe, the majority coming from England, Scotland, Wales and Ireland. Maori are the next largest ethnic group, followed by Pacific Islanders, who comprise nearly 4 percent of the population. The central role played by the church in the life of Pacific Islanders has been reflected in New Zealand since the 1960s. Islanders in New Zealand have in some cases retained their links with their home churches while in others they have joined New Zealand denominations. In 1969 when the Congregational Union merged with the Presbyterian Church, many Islanders in New Zealand became Presbyterians. Others, such as those who were members of the Congregational Christian Church of Samoa, remained part of the Samoan church. There are also a number of independent Islander churches.

The desire to maintain language, culture and identity — always important for migrants in a new context — is seen in the Islander churches. It has not always been easy for them to retain their distinctive ethos. That becomes even more difficult with the pressures placed on New Zealand-born Pacific Islanders, who are caught between the world their parents have come from and the one in which they live. In the islands, people lived in village communities where people were related to one another and in which the church was central. In New Zealand most Islanders are scattered in urban communities where the majority of people do not attend church. Their children are influenced by secular values propagated by television and attitudes towards authority and Sunday observance which run counter to island standards.

Islander churches have been successful in developing vibrant worshipping communities, but are faced with the challenge of passing their faith and customs on to their children's children. For Islanders who are members of the New Zealand Presbyterian and Methodist Churches it has not always been easy learning *Palangi* (European) ways of doing things. In order to meet their needs, Islanders have been requesting and gaining more autonomy over their own church affairs.

New Zealand has had small Chinese and Indian populations for many years. At the turn of the century blatantly racist attitudes towards them found expression in discriminatory legislation. The Presbyterian Church developed work among the Chinese with ministers in Auckland and Dunedin for their communities. The arrival of Asian migrants in the 1980s and 1990s from Korea, Hong Kong, Taiwan, Malaysia and other areas has presented new challenges to the churches and the community. In 1995 some 2 percent of the population was of Asian origin.

The growing ethnic diversity of New Zealand's population has resulted in a growing multicultural society. Race relations and human-rights legislation outlaw discrimination on the basis of race, religion, gender, sexual preference or marital status. The development of a multicultural society, however, is not without its strains. For Maori there is a concern that their historical and traditional rights as *tangata whenua* will be marginalized by the competing concerns of other ethnic minorities. While recognizing the rights of others to preserve their language and culture, Maori point out that other people can always go to the places from which they came, where their language and culture continue to be used. That is not an option for Maori, for Aotearoa New Zealand is their home, where their language and culture are rooted and where it grows or dies.

Within the Maori world and the wider society there is a great debate over *tino rangatiratanga* (sovereignty). In the

Maori text of the treaty of Waitangi *tino rangatiratanga* over their lands and possessions was guaranteed to chiefs. The issue facing Aotearoa New Zealand as it approaches the new millennium is how this sovereignty is to be understood and expressed. This is part of a global debate on the rights of indigenous peoples. For some, sovereignty means the establishment of a nation within the nation. For others, it means Maori having autonomy to control their own affairs. The churches, particularly Anglicans and Methodists, have tried to balance partnership and autonomy.

Churches play an important role enabling people from different cultures to meet and listen to one another. That is not always easy. People like to worship in their own way and in their own language. Multicultural congregations have to work hard at both affirming the ethnic identity of the variety of groups that make up their membership and finding ways in which people can cross over cultural boundaries. Multicultural denominations, with their distinctive ethnic congregations, have to be open to finding different ways of meeting and doing their business.

These cultural tensions mirror in many ways the theological diversity which is found among those who call themselves Christians. Within some churches this theological diversity is more pronounced, with people variously labelled as radical, liberal, evangelical, conservative and fundamentalist being found within the one denomination. In other cases denominations are more clearly identified with one part of the theological spectrum. Pentecostal and charismatic influences have resulted in alliances being formed across denominational boundaries with people who have shared similar experiences. Theological coalitions of like-minded people have emerged, with people often finding that they have more in common with people from other denominations than with some within their own.

Ecumenical forces, which sought to bring the churches together, have diminished in the late 20th century, resulting in greater inter- and intra-denominational polarity. The issue of ordaining and recognizing the leadership of homosexuals has become a divisive issue in some denominations. Underlying this have been widely divergent views on the authority of scripture and how it should be interpreted, understood and applied within a late 20th-century context. The nature of the church and its self-understanding have also been under question. For some the church is an exclusive community which defines itself over against the world and sets rigid boundaries, marking off heresy from orthodoxy, member from non-member. For others the church is an inclusive community of pilgrims who are on a journey in which they attempt to bring together the history and traditions they have inherited within their contemporary context. Both these descriptions are in some senses caricatures but they do point to a long-standing tensionwithin Christianity: is it in the world yet not of the world, or is it in the world and of the world?

The bicultural relationships within the New Zealand churches, the multicultural challenge facing both church and society and the issues regarding the exclusive or inclusive nature of the church, are fundamentally questions of ecclesiology. The understanding of the nature, being and purpose of the church are critical questions as the church faces a new millennium. The relationship between gospel and culture is critical at this point in helping shape the church for its missiological purpose.

NOTES

[1] *New Zealand Herald*, 7 February 1990.
[2] Figures are based on the *New Zealand Official Year Book 95*, Auckland, Statistics New Zealand, 1995.
[3] R.D. Rakena, "Methodists among the Maori", in J.G. Udy and E.G. Clancy, eds, *Dig or Die*, Sydney, World Methodist Historical Society, 1981, p.227.
[4] *Minutes of Annual Conference of the Methodist Church*, 1983, p.665.

6. *Endings and Beginnings*

In November 1986 when Pope John Paul II visited Auckland, a Maori carving was displayed on the platform in a prominent place beside him. The carving was of Mary holding Jesus. Unlike the typical European representation of the Madonna and child, Mary has a "full facial tattoo... traditionally used on a man". Its use in this instance signified "that the woman was a virgin. In earlier times, some highborn women were set aside and not allowed to marry or be touched by men, and their status was made clear by a full facial tattoo." Both Mary and Jesus are tattooed over their whole bodies.

The carving was originally presented to Roman Catholic authorities in 1845 by a converted Maori carver at Maketu for use in a new church. The carving, however, was rejected, probably because it was thought "unsuitable, perhaps even irreverent... Those early missionaries saw only what would be to them a pagan carving perpetuating primitive superstitious beliefs. They failed to appreciate the spirituality of the *tangata whenua*." What was intended to enhance a church was presented to the Auckland Museum in 1901.[1]

This story is a reminder that our way of seeing the world is shaped by our own preconceptions. What was rejected in 1845 has become a priceless *taonga* (treasure), symbolizing the process of indigenization which has accompanied the gospel wherever it has encountered a new cultural context. The encounter between Pakeha and Maori brought different worlds, cultures, traditions and customs into contact with one another, giving rise to new worlds. The interaction of missionaries and Maori, Christianity and Maori religion and customs, was a dynamic process as Maori incorporated Christian teaching and biblical ideas within their own worldview. Sadly the missionaries often saw themselves as those who had something to give which Maori needed, rather than as people who could also receive from Maori. Missionaries learnt the Maori language and lived alongside Maori, establishing close bonds of friendship with many. There is little evidence, however, of missionaries taking back within their own culture insights from the Maori world.

The reconceptualizing of Christianity within their own culture was something which Maori undertook themselves in ways which met their own needs. The biblical stories about bondage in Egypt, deliverance through the Exodus, the wanderings in the wilderness, the entry into and conquest of the promised land provided very rich imagery for a people who experienced oppression throughout the 19th century. The loss of land, the impact of disease and the pressure of Pakeha settlement led Maori to make their own responses by themselves bringing together the biblical, Maori and European worlds.

Missionary Christianity in the mainline churches tried to absorb Maori within Pakeha structures. The resilience of Maori culture and identity has not allowed this to happen, and in the late 20th century Maori Christianity is asserting its own character within the denominations. In the Anglican Church this has been seen not only in the restructuring of the church but also in the way in which Maori have taken responsibility for becoming bearers of the gospel among their own people. The use of the Maketu carving of Madonna and child during the Pope's visit and the Anglican Prayer Book with its bilingual liturgies are evidence of a growing maturity in the whole church towards Maori culture. The gospel seed has taken root in the soil of Aotearoa and has given rise to different varieties of Christianity which both indicate their gospel origins and the context from which they come.

For the Pakeha church the task of reconceptualizing the gospel has really become possible only in the late 20th century. The colonizing process of transplantation meant that the first generation of migrants and their children and grandchildren retained what was familiar: dependence on imported traditions was important in helping people sing the Lord's song in a strange land. But the land is no longer strange and people are tentatively beginning to sing the gospel in ways which reflect the seasons, geography and place in which they live. The Pohutukawa, found along the coastline arching out over the sea, with dark green foliage and its brilliant red flower which blooms in December, has become a symbol for the Advent season. The dolphin found in New Zealand's waterways, "the sailor's friend", has been used by one hymn-writer as an image for Christ: "be the dolphin Christ; lead us on to eternity".[2] Other indigenous examples could be given from art, poetry and literature. Some might see these images as of little consequence. Christianity, however, throughout its history has expressed its universality within particular contexts as people in each time and each place express their faith in ways which are authentic for them.

The colonial past is over, but the legacy which it has left cannot be ignored. That is seen in the way in which Aotearoa New Zealand is facing up to and trying to deal with the grievances of Maori which originate in the injustices of the past. The church was both directly and indirectly part of this process and has been seeking to put its own house in order. But the church also offers to the community a tradition which offers healing and reconciliation when justice, love and mercy are brought together.

In undertaking its ministry within New Zealand society the church has contributed much through its pastoral concern and in its meeting of human need. The difficulty of sustaining a prophetic witness has been noted. Significant individuals and groups have, out of Christian concern, addressed issues of exploitation, racism, war, nuclear armaments and economic injustice. Churches are having to come to terms with their minority and even marginal status in society. Christendom is dead and churches are no longer in the position to impose their moral agendas on society. As witnesses to the gospel and its values, however, churches are now better placed to preach and embody the redeeming love of God.

The churches find themselves as minority groups in a society which is highly secularized, driven by materialistic values and apathetic if not antagonistic to formalized institutional religion. There is, however, a great interest in diverse expressions of spirituality, ranging from the Pentecostal and charismatic renewal expressed in the Toronto Blessing to the Creation Spirituality associated with Matthew Fox and through a whole range of New Age religious movements. The dependence on imported theologies and ecclesiastical structures which marked much of the history of the church in Aotearoa New Zealand is also found in this religious imitation. New Zealand culture is very eclectic and very vulnerable to the influences of the latest fad or guru.

These chapters have examined the interaction between gospel and culture in Aotearoa New Zealand largely in terms of the history of the country, its churches and its peoples. The classical categories used by H. Richard Niebuhr could easily be applied to exegete this history. The critique of Western culture offered by Lesslie Newbigin and others has also found expression in New Zealand. Harold Turner, a New Zealander who gained an international reputation as an authority on the new religious movements resulting from the interaction of Christian missionaries with indigenous cultures, has in retirement headed up the Gospel and Cultures Trust in New Zealand. Turner has argued for the need for what he has called "Deep Mission" to the roots of New Zealand culture. This takes account of the pervasive influence of Western culture on the shaping of New Zealand identity and the need for the gospel to be freed from the shackles of the Christendom attitudes and Enlightenment thinking which were transplanted by both missionaries and the settler church. Turner calls for the "de-indigenizing of the Christian faith within New Zealand before we can think of genuine indigenization. The basic reason why the gospel has so little impact in this country is that it has lost its distinctiveness by assimilation to the prevailing culture within which we all live."[3]

New Zealand society has undergone dramatic shifts as it has struggled to become tolerant and inclusive. The denominational divisions of the last century and the racial attitudes towards nonwhite people can no longer be sustained. The presence of Maori as *tangata whenua* and of Pakeha descended from European migrants, and the influx of Pacific Islanders, Asians and others, have created a complex multicultural society in which people are learning to live with diversity. For the churches, living with diversity has never been easy. Their identification with middle-class values and the alienation of most of the working class from active involvement in the churches' life have often turned the churches themselves into social ghettos. Theological polarization and divisions, for example over issues of sexuality, have created tensions which churches struggle to contain. The equal participation of women and men in all aspects of the life of the church is in the process of resolution in some churches but there are still many obstacles to overcome.

As the churches approach the new millennium there is a need for ecclesiological rethinking in terms of these questions:
— What does the church exist for?
— Whom does the church exist for?
— What gospel does the church preach?
— How does the church preach its gospel?

The development of the churches in Aotearoa New Zealand and the interaction of gospel and culture, like all human stories, are made up of successes and failures. Often the negative aspects have stood out more clearly than the positive ones. It is all too easy to overlook the faithful dedication and service of the many thousands who have lived their lives by the standards of the gospel as they have understood them. In pointing to the negative dimensions of the churches' role in New Zealand's history the purpose has not been to denigrate but to illuminate what has been, in the hope that this will enable people to see more clearly what could be the way for the future. All endings are beginnings, and so this booklet ends with the hope that in undertaking their mission in Aotearoa New Zealand the churches will learn from their past as they seek to understand and embody the gospel within their cultures and context.

NOTES

[1] *Accent*, March 1987, p.32.
[2] Colin Gibson, *With One Voice*, Hymn 672.
[3] Harold Turner, "The Three Levels of Mission in New Zealand", in Bruce Patrick, ed., *New Vision New Zealand: Calling the Whole Church to take the Whole Gospel to the Whole Nation*, Auckland, Vision New Zealand, 1993, p.67.